Find Your Voice™

A Methodology for Enhancing Literacy Through Re-Writing and Re-Acting

Gail Noppe-Brandon

HEINEMANN
Portsmouth, NH

Heinemann

A division of Reed Elsevier Inc.

361 Hanover Street

Portsmouth, NH 03801–3912

www.heinemanndrama.com

Offices and agents throughout the world

Library of Congress Cataloging-in-Publication Data

Noppe-Brandon, Gail.

    Find your voice : a methodology for enhancing literacy through re-writing and re-acting / Gail Noppe-Brandon.

      p. cm.

    ISBN 0-325-00701-2 (alk. paper)

    1. English language—Rhetoric—Study and teaching. 2. English language—Composition and exercises—Study and teaching. 3. Playwriting—Study and teaching. 4. Drama in education. 5. Language arts. I. Title.

PE1404.N665 2004

808'.042'071—dc22   2004010060

Editor: Lisa A. Barnett

Production editor: Sonja S. Chapman

Cover design: Catherine Hawkes, Cat & Mouse

Compositor: Gina Poirier, Gina Poirier Design

Manufacturing: Steve Bernier

Printed in the United States of America on acid-free paper

08 07 06 05 04 PAH 1 2 3 4 5

For Jesse and Geordy

May you always speak your minds,
and your hearts.

Contents

Acknowledgments

S o many wonderful people have been a part of this twenty-year journey; I especially want to thank the following: First and foremost Dr. Paul Reisch, for teaching me to believe in my own ability to learn. Dr. Jerry Surasky, for teaching me to trust. Charles Kakatsakis, for teaching me to enjoy being seen. Also Jack Lee, Joyce Hall, Joy Kellman, and Milan Stit, for being such extraordinary Coaches. Julia Miles, Robert Moss, Gary Garrison, Michael Warren Powell, Nancy Quinn, and Wynn Handman, for encouraging my art-making. And Leon Felder, for teaching me about fear management.

For their support of my teaching in its earliest incarnation: New York University Dean Steven Currey, and former Dean Jill N. Claster. Also Professor Perry Meisel, for teaching me about text analysis; Professor Sydney Mailick, for supporting my belief that things can be changed from within; and Professor Dennis Donohue, for encouraging my fascination with Clustering through the work of W. B. Yeats.

At the Children's Aid Society: Phil Coltoff, Pete Moses, Betsy Mayberry, T. Jewett, Barbara Ternes, Ruby Dreyer, and Nick Scopetta, for allowing me the space to grow this idea.

The key colleagues who made so many discoveries with me, and worked so hard for me: my trusted partner and artistic associate Rose Olivito; and my first two gifted Company dramaturges, Laura Castro and Jeanette Horn. Also Michael Schwartz, Rita Kogler, Mark McCullough, Shana Burns, Arden Kirkland, Daisy Taylor, Jenny Bruce, Andrea Sperling, and Nancy Paris—artists who brought so much to our early productions.

The network of professionals who helped me to bring this methodology to so many young people in need: Ellen Kirshbaum, Sonnet Takahisa, Shelly Alpert, Pat Wosley, Gussie Kappner, Steve Stoll, Ria Grosvenor, Julie Beck, John Hoffman, Prep for Prep, Sharon Dunne, Young Audiences, and The Children's Museum of Manhattan.

For their support of the program: some of my first Advisory Board members, Greg McCaslin, Erica Ress and Michele Lowe. My later Board of Directors and Patrons for continuing support: Bernice Stern, Beth Rudin DeWoody and the Rudin Family, Leah Krauss of the New York Community Trust, Marilynn Donini of Philip Morris, John Morning, Martha Tuck Rozett, Carl and Betty Pforzheimer, The Rockefeller Foundation, The Carnegie Corporation of New York, Alliance of Resident Theaters/New York, the late Suzanne Usdan of the Lemberg Foundation, The Tiger Woods Foundation, Michael Bloomberg, New York State Council on the Arts, Murray and Belle Nathan, The Pinkerton Foundation, The Heckscher Foundation, The Auchincloss Foundation, Agnes Gund, The New York Times Foundation, Michael Margitich, and Pentacle's Foundation for Independent Artists. And the rest of my current Board members: Louise Hutchins Bryant, Joyce Eichenberg, Diane Genovesi, Kathy Lopez, Brian Healy, Judith Bendewald, Jamie Bennett, Maggie Brown, Dr. Eduardo Martí, and Ron Sirak.

Michael Lennon, Esq., for years of wise counsel and patience. Jill Yablon and Colm Davis—two school teachers who stepped into my shoes and enabled me to take a year off to write this book. Chotsani Sackey and Tanya Tatum, for assisting me with the preparation of this manuscript; and my editor, Lisa Barnett, who is herself a brilliant Guiding Voice.

Most important, the National Endowment for the Arts and Susan Petersmeyer of the Petersmeyer Family Foundation, for giving me the opportunity to write this book.

Each and every one of my students—young and old—for trusting me so much, and teaching me so much.

My mother, Adele Noppe, who changed her life so that I could attend LaGuardia High School for the Arts; and Gangadei Bacchus who guarded and loved my young children while I wrote this book.

My vigilant and insightful readers: Lucy Matos, Amatullah King, and Melissa Rocha.

My lifelong muses, Georgia O'Keefe and Virginia Woolf, who taught me that if I really looked I could see a whole world inside of one flower, and could explore a whole life in one single day. God, indeed, is in the details.

And my beloved husband Scott, who has always encouraged my dreams. Two years ago he said the three most important words I could ever have hoped to hear: "Write, write, write!"

*If you have butterflies in your stomach,
invite them into your heart.*

Introduction: Losing Your Voice

*T*he *Find Your Voice™ methodology* outlined in this book is designed to help students conquer their fear of *public sharing* and to help them become more literate. By *literate*, I'm not referring to their ability to recognize and decipher letters and symbols but to their ability to communicate effectively, and to effectively receive the communication of others. To help them accomplish this, I use *re-acting* and *re-writing* as tools to improve students' reading, writing, speaking, and listening skills. I use *fear management* to make it safe enough for students to acquire them. Based on my twenty-year track record of successful *Coaching*, the book is primarily geared toward English teachers, who remain on the frontline in the battle against inarticulation. But, it's also intended for use by teachers of *all* subjects. Even when students raise their hands in a math class, they are sharing publicly. The Find Your Voice™ methodology has been used in private programs, in after-school programs, and in college and public school academic classes. However it is used, the goal is to improve communication—to strengthen voices.

I firmly believe that above and beyond acquisition of the basic skills, we must be *taught* from a young age to have faith in expressions of ourselves. But this kind of faith is not easy to endow! Most people are a little afraid to *really* communicate with another person. Whether as a speaker or a listener, communication requires a degree of intimacy, and intimacy requires trust; and *trust has to be earned.* In a classroom of thirty students that's headed by a teacher whose communication skills may also be weak, trust is rarely earned. I've found this to be particularly true when the majority of students come from homes where no one listens and no one encourages them to speak. With good reason, these students always fear that they won't be well received. Any expression of themselves— whether it's a memorized fact or an imaginatively interpreted idea— makes students very vulnerable. This is why *public speaking* is the number one *fear.*

Finding Your Voice

In the beginning there is fear, and that's what prevents most everyone from communicating well. If we're best at helping others conquer those things that have bedeviled us the most, I was drawn to the work of finding voices because I was born into the legacy of shyness. I have had the opportunity to observe many varieties of shyness and, after (two decades of) helping young people to grapple with it, have come to the conclusion that it's largely a fear of *negative response.* It seems to me that several factors can contribute to people's development of this fear: Some are just more sensitive to the reactions of others; some had overly judgmental parents; and others are simply born with a perfectionist temperament, which makes them harder on themselves. Or all three! Whatever the factors, they render communication painful.

Keeping silent is often just a way of avoiding that pain; however, where there is avoidance, there is also *shame.* While all young people feel pain and shame at some time, many learn to keep *silent all the time*—essentially, they become *voiceless.* Some discover ways to express themselves privately by writing poetry, drawing pictures, making music, or acting out stories. They explore every possible way to "leak" out their voice in dribs and drabs. But many remain totally voiceless both at home and at school and, over time, their ability to connect with the world is compromised. These students usually either act out; or they "act in" by hiding behind a detached affect, under headphones, within jargon, or surrounded by a wall. They become what I have dubbed *communicatively disabled.*

This disability can demonstrate itself in a variety of ways, including functional illiteracy, academic failure, depression, social alienation, and even hyperactivity and the overdiagnosed Attention Deficit Disorder. Ironically, I have seen the same factors result in the opposite of shyness—a kind of inappropriate extraversion, often perceived as *insensitivity* to others. I believe that this is because people who have never really been listened to are usually incapable of listening to others. Although they may appear to have a voice, it's not an authentic one—not one that can express their true selves. At bottom they share the same fear of connection that the shy person possesses—the flip side of the coin. And when you're afraid to connect, and we all are under certain circumstances, you require a special kind of teaching.

This is why acting, or more accurately *re-acting*, when it is taught well, can be so helpful to people with communication disorders. As scary as it sounds to *non-actors*, good acting is simply about listening, connecting, and *wanting* an authentic response. Good acting is *not* about overemoting, showing off, or wearing masks; it is about the *removal* of masks. This is why actors train long and hard to achieve their craft. They must fine-tune their instrument to ensure that they are comfortable with every expression of themselves. If they are afraid to express anger, sadness, or joy, it will be evident in their characterization of someone else. And, if these feelings were never tolerated by their loved ones, they most certainly *will be afraid* to express them. They will be like pianos that are missing half of their keys; how can such an instrument play? Obviously, part of it will always remain silent.

I was one of the shy kids who enjoyed private expressions of myself. It wasn't until I began to learn the crafts of acting and playwriting, as a young adult, that I found my voice. Acting taught me to listen, and playwriting taught me to talk, because plays are public conversations. This is why I often teach the various forms of expression as an *integrated approach.*

I have spent a long time building my craft in these disciplines, and I have been able to grow into a communicator. I have also come to believe that fear management must play a role in the work of *finding* a voice. However, my methodology for doing so *is not to be confused* with therapy or social work. I *never* discuss or meddle in the lives, memories, or personal dramas of students. The therapeutic value comes from the discipline and nurturing involved in the successful attainment of the craft. My teaching focuses only on the lives of the characters that are being enacted or written about. However, although the focus never appears to be personal, who we really are is always discernible from our acting and writing choices. Shaping these choices helps us to understand and to shape ourselves.

As I went on to find *my voice,* and to eventually start a *Company* of my own, I understood that I had been given the gift of a second chance. I had gone from being an inaudible child who never raised her hand at school, to comfortably speaking before crowds of hundreds and Coaching others past their own shyness; from never crying or expressing anger in public, to acting with a full range of character-appropriate emotions onstage and offstage; from never telling the secrets of my own struggles, to writing plays that helped others understand their own; from being voiceless to being vocal. So, I wanted to give that same gift to others.

Everyone I know has felt either unheard or inarticulate at some time. Not everyone wants or needs to become a theatre artist, but everyone I know has some fears about and perceives limitations in their ability to articulate themselves. And everyone I know has things they'd like to tell. I've observed that we all thrive when someone invites us to tell it—especially if the inviter can also teach us *how to tell it well.* As a young adult, I was fortunate to have a series of great teachers and guides. They demonstrated to me that the best teaching happens when teachers and students form *learning relationships.*

For me, school was a place to wait out the day until the real creative explorations could occur in after-school arts classes and through imaginative play with friends. My early teachers made no attempts to understand my learning style and were not equipped to help me fight what I have come to call *communication demons.* I sat, like so many schoolchildren do today, wishing to be invisible. I see them all the time in classrooms citywide, refusing to remove their jackets—wrapped in a cocoon of self-protection. There used to be twenty-five of us crammed into a sterile learning space; now there can be upwards of thirty. Many students tune-out long before they are ever expected to read and write proficiently; essentially they've become nonlearners—the doors are shut.

The first time that *my door* really began to unlock was when my LaGuardia High School homeroom teacher took an interest in my learning. Being the gifted teacher that he was, he sensed that my shyness belied a deeper desire to connect. However, like the disaffected students that I described previously, he could see that I was locked inside myself. The key that he provided wasn't only his knowledge, which was vast, but also the personal *interest* that he invested, and his belief that I was a worthwhile investment. He became *my ally,* and then he became my English teacher. Through his passion for his subject, and his caring attention, I fell in love with academic learning for the first time in my life.

I had finally found a *guide* and this guide gently led me through the experience of taking others in and allowing their knowledge to change me. That teacher also led me, through his incredibly high standards, to the belief in my own *ability* to excel. He became someone in the school environment who recognized and applauded my accomplishments, and someone to turn to when school got too overwhelming and stressful. It may sound like he invested an inordinate amount of time guiding me, but he didn't. He invested the time it took *to look* into my eyes *each day*—to really *see me*. He invested the time to invite me to participate when my voice was failing me. He invested the time to assign, and then really read, a poem that revealed my authentic self. That teacher invested his ability to comment on the quality of that poem while essentially ignoring, in a good way, the content. He personalized school for me and, in doing so, taught me everything I have needed to know about great teaching.

After high school I spent many years attempting to replicate an environment where learning was personal, teaching was passionate, and standards were high. I didn't find it. I succeeded academically only because I had learned how to learn, but I didn't thrive. As young adults, when we move away from our homes and families, our worlds become even larger. As a college student, I rediscovered how crucial it is that the teaching environment offer *relationship-based learning— Coaching*. When that was offered, students thrived, and those professors were usually the recipients of the "Great Teacher" awards on their respective campuses; but, they were rare indeed. Like many others, I resorted to private expressions again, and the public voice that had begun to emerge went back underground. It remained there until several years later. Two things then happened simultaneously: I began to study, and to teach, re-acting and re-writing. These endeavors fed and supported one another and led to the development of my Coaching style.

When I went on to graduate school, I built my craft as a creative writer and an analyst of text. At the same time, I was asked to teach this craft to others. The salient difference between me and my first-year college students was that I knew that I loved to write, and they knew that they didn't! Rather than relying on the adages of the Expository Writing textbooks, I attempted to emulate my high school mentor by teaching through passion for my subject, placing great demands on the learner and *connection*. The more I taught the more I learned about teaching. I was so successful at getting resistant learners to find joy and craft in reading, writing, and speaking, that I was asked to teach in a special program for bright but underachieving students. I had come full circle around to myself.

Without even being conscious of it, I began to override my students' communication disorders through a connected style of teaching. This is not to say that I knew very much about their personal lives, or the particular issues that led to their *voicelessness*. I focused only on their work, guiding them toward the attainment of craft through motivation and responsiveness. I was shocked at my own results. The most seemingly inarticulate young people morphed into writers and actors. I began to believe students were all secret geniuses, capable of attaining skill at anything—a belief that I continue to cultivate.

It was in this college classroom, twenty years ago, that the seeds of my Find Your Voice™ methodology were sown. Borrowing in unintended ways from all of the mentors who had guided me, I seemed to have stumbled on one possible antidote to the state that we perceive as *illiteracy*. In the case of many of my students, I was the first person in their lives who really listened to what they had to say. I was also the first person who encouraged them to speak in their authentic voices. They trusted me, and apparently that made all the difference.

At the same time, I began to study with a gifted psychologist. During our first meeting, I shared many of my insights about the causes of my voicelessness. He informed me that it was not these insights alone that would help me, but the development of a *trusting relationship* with him—he was right. During my training, I was empowered by the knowledge that I could say anything and he would *listen and respond* authentically—consistently. As I articulated things that had been previously verboten, I grew increasingly more comfortable speaking and writing publicly. This was the opportunity that I offered to my students as well.

I also began to study with a gifted acting teacher whose mantra was: *"No acting, please."* His absolute insistence on simple, connected, authentic work shaped a small army of actors who were fortunate enough to study with him; and it drove others out of the business. I observed some of the most seasoned performers in the class resist, dissolve, and then improve under his directive to *connect*—to stop "acting for their own enjoyment." As he urged them to make the scene or monologue "about the *other* person," I realized that even the most seemingly uninhibited people can lack the courage to really communicate. It was only through their trust in him that all of the students, the inaudible and the brash alike, found the ability to connect. And it was the combined wisdom of both of these two guides that I brought back to my classroom, where I encouraged students to write freely on their first drafts, and then to use their re-writes for shaping, honing, and ultimately presenting an authentic piece.

Although they initially balked at the thought of writing or enacting a play, I assured students that it was not my purpose to get them agents or to help them book TV commercials. I explained that this was simply a *skill-building* exercise that would be practiced in the sanctity of our classroom, with the utmost respect and support of one another (see Chapter Two, *The Learning Environment: Orientation*). These assurances made it *doable*, but it certainly did not eradicate their fear. Fortunately, one of my goals was to demonstrate what they could accomplish *despite* their fear. I can remember the first time *I* got up to perform a monologue. Not even the people in the first row could hear me, and that's the way I wanted it. There was nothing wrong with my vocal chords, and I had tons of energy; I was simply not ready to give up my inaudibility. I still needed permission to articulate myself.

Fortunately, my acting teacher had the skill to make it safe for me to do so. Without ever ridiculing my shyness, he led me, like leading a kitten with a bowl of milk, toward my voice. And he did so by constantly focusing on my scene partners: How they were responding to me, what I wanted from them, and how I could get it from them. In this way he took the spotlight off me. He earned the trust of his students through the clarity of his beliefs, and his unwavering commitment to *battling* our demons. Like all young people who have hidden parts of themselves away, after getting kudos for allowing myself to be seen and heard I eventually began to drop my defenses. Then I began to communicate. As a public writer, I was always able to imitate or critique anyone else's style; now I wanted to share my stories.

My next great mentor was a playwriting teacher who also encouraged me to write with all of the keys on my "instrument." Like my other guides, he knew his craft inside out. He challenged me, while making it safe for me to not already know. Plus, he learned enough about my style of learning to make it personal. He saw a gifted private writer in me, and helped me to find the courage to *go public*. He did this by giving me finite and specific assignments, which allowed me to override my inner censor long enough to begin writing. This teacher understood well that a white page is the most intimidating color of all. To get me started all it took was his suggestion of a character, place, and circumstance, such as two old men sitting on a park bench. My imagination was hooked—I wanted to connect the dots. Then he focused me on the very exacting exercise of *revision*, including "raising the stakes," strengthening continuity, eliminating repetition and exposition, and simplifying language (see Chapter Four, *The Methodology: Writing and Re-Writing*). As he pushed *my characters* to speak authentically, I began to reveal more and more.

Much the same as a Rorschach inkblot, having an assignment to respond to alleviates the guilt about beginning to talk, and it reveals what you really want to talk *about*. If the two old men on your bench are both dying of cancer, death is clearly on your mind. If they are old friends reunited after a long separation, betrayal or the desire for for-giveness might be an important issue. If they witness a mugging, fear of physical danger might be lurking. But, the *reasons* for the choices don't matter—the focus must remain on communicating a story well. I once heard Stephen Sondheim asked about how he thought up the ideas for his enormous output. He answered: "If someone asked me to write a love song, I couldn't do it. But if they asked me to write a love song about a woman at a bar wearing a red dress, that I could do with no trouble." Even he needed help to *begin*. When I first started teaching writing, I instinctively decided to have my students respond to photographs; it was very effective. Years later, with the benefit of twenty–twenty hindsight, I could fully see the benefits of this choice.

When I look back at the team of Coaches who helped me to find my voice, I recall an illustration from Jonathan Swift's *Gulliver's Travels:* He was being tied up by an army of Lilliputians. In my case, the Lilliputians were *untying* me. So many people worked so hard, for so long, to pull my voice out of me. How wonderful it would have been if the help had come sooner, before my voice was so severely lodged in my throat. If communication had been part and parcel of my education from the beginning, I could have been a full participant in a process that sadly left me out. This is what I have dedicated myself to doing for others. But the number of communicatively illiterate young people is growing, and the number of teachers with the ability to connect seems to be shrinking.

Because I can only train a few hundred students directly each year, I have turned my energy to the dissemination of a process that has worked unfailingly for people of all ages and backgrounds, dur-ing and after school, in theatres and social service organizations, in workshops that ran for a full year or for only three weeks, or once a week during an *Advisory* period. Users of this book's guidelines will not necessarily have had simultaneous acting and writing training, but teachers and learners of all levels and subjects can benefit from the fact that I did. It was the synergy of these pursuits that led to the methodology that I call *Find Your Voice*™. If you are reading this book, it's probably because a part of you is mute, or because you want to help others to find their voices—or both. Read on.

How I Found Five Hundred Voices 1

*I*t's been my experience that in order for someone to learn to communicate, they must feel safe, secure, and encouraged. In fact I have come to believe that teaching noncommunicators to communicate requires a very special kind of intervention; the purpose of the intervention is not to *inform* students, but to *transform* them. This is a great responsibility, and it can only be accomplished if trust is established first. To establish trust, I believe that a teacher must:

- Know the subject well—confidence inspires confidence.
- Have great enthusiasm for the subject—passion is contagious.
- Have the desire to learn about how students learn, or why they don't learn, *before* attempting to transform them.
- Help students understand how the transformation will occur.
- Convey to students why becoming more communicative will be useful to them.
- Practice, above all, being an *ally* in the process, not a judge.

Managing Fear: The Journey From Inarticulation to Articulation

I had many surprises at the start of my twenty-year pursuit of finding voices. Not the least of these was the discovery that many young people don't like to read. And, if they were never introduced to reading as a source of pleasure, they also lacked the desire to write. For these students, reading and writing were strictly school-based activities. I actually consider them to be social skills. When I was first called on to teach a required Expository Writing course at New York University, I asked the following questions on the first day of the term:

1. "How many of you like to read?" (Out of twenty-eight students, no more than eight hands went up, and some of those meant strictly comic-book reading.)
2. "How many of you like to write?" (Maybe two or three hands went up, and at least one of those students was just angling to get a decent grade.)

Among those who raised their hands, few *chose* to read or write, they simply didn't mind it. As a formerly *voiceless* person, who had channeled many of my own thoughts and feelings into private writing, I couldn't totally understand this. It was only as I closed the gap between my private and public expressions that I began to fully appreciate the *vulnerability* involved in revealing things, even to oneself.

That first time I taught I looked out at a sea of already indifferent faces, and wondered what I could possibly say to engage those students. Lots of barely learned rules about grammar and composition floated through my head, along with memories of my own half-invented book reports. I couldn't really blame the class for being disaffected. I wanted my students to learn to love reading and writing, and to be able to do both well, but my instincts told me that I would have to take them beyond their previous experience of school to achieve that. On the spur of the moment, I decided not to recommend the required text. I also opted not to distribute the departmental syllabus. I simply took attendance, taking the time to really look at and to interact with each student so that I would remember their names for the second class. I was damned if any of my students would feel the kind of invisibility that I had known. My instinct turned out to be a good one. At the second meeting, I looked at each student and greeted them by name, and I could sense some tension in them ease. I didn't yet know it, but that was my first giant step into *relationship-based* teaching.

Now that they had my attention, and I had theirs, I began to build on the bit of trust that had been established by our greeting. I hung a print of an Andrew Wyeth painting on the board, and then circulated small copies of it to each student. I had never done a *free-write* in my life, I was simply following my heart. I'd always loved that particular painting: It captured a lace curtain blowing through an open window and seemed to set the stage for an event without dictating it. I asked the students to study the picture; then, I asked them to make up a story about something that had happened, or was about to happen, in that room. I told them to write whatever came into their heads for ten minutes, and that the only incorrect response was a blank page. After a brief stunned silence, I was astonished to hear every pen in the room begin to scratch away enthusiastically. Not one of these self-proclaimed haters of writing was finished ten minutes later when I asked them to stop.

I invited several volunteers to read their pieces aloud. We were all struck by the number of *echoes* we heard from piece to piece. Although there were no figures in the painting, several students wrote about a dying grandparent. And, although there were no clocks in the picture either, the word *time* came up in almost all of them. I knew that I had just witnessed a phenomenon. I collected the remaining stories, and read them privately after class. The grammar and syntax were almost uniformly horrific. Also, because I had invited them to override their internal censors, as is always the case with free-writing, they contained more than a little profanity. However, they all had *some* dramatic or poetic element worth developing.

I gave each student extensive written feedback, primarily in the form of questions. My questions were focused on how their stories could "open out" to reveal more about the people who inhabited the world they'd created. I also asked them to explore what the relationship between these people might be, by encouraging them to discover some potential conflicts. Finally, I asked them to create an outline for a story. I would learn, years later, that in the film business this is called a *"Treatment."* Oddly enough, I even encouraged them to try watching the story play out like a movie in their imaginations. Because they were all film and television lovers, this was a notion that resonated. Getting them to put the idea on paper was the tricky part.

If they showed up at all, many of the students showed up at the next meeting unprepared. Their communication phobias had made it too difficult for them to write anything formal. I quickly discovered that absenteeism, lateness, and unpreparedness directly reflect terror. The fear management inherent in the Find Your Voice™ methodology, which I developed later, was designed to address this tendency. I decided to go around the room and have those students who had written, share their Treatment ideas verbally. This choice offered other surprising opportunities.

Because the students couldn't see each other in their rows of seats, and because I instinctively knew how crucial *eye contact* would be for enhancing communication, I had them move their chairs into a circle formation. I can't emphasize enough the importance of this shift. Even now, twenty years later, my former students still speak about the "circle" when referring to my classes. I have come to think of it as an Aristotelian kind of *learning circle* in which we are all both teachers and learners of each other. I also see it as a big metaphoric *embrace* in which we are surrounded, buffered, supported, and generally appreciated. (The only time this circle is broken is during the acting classes. At that time, I use a semicircle, with the *gap* becoming a playing area for the two students who are working—see Chapter Two, *The Learning Environment: Orientation*.) Another opportunity that the verbal sharing afforded was that each participant got to use his or her voice during class, however briefly, within a safe and encouraging dialogue with the teacher. The absentees got to do it alone with me on the phone—a time-consuming, short-term sacrifice that yielded an enormous long-term gain.

After these exchanges everyone had a workable idea for two characters, as well as a potential conflict between them. I then invited them to go home and let the characters start talking to each other in *dialogue* form, with a particular want in mind. I knew that their first attempts at writing dialogue might be a little clunky, but we all speak in the form of dialogue all day long. Not unlike actors learning how to behave naturally onstage, all writers can be *taught* to speak naturally on paper. And because most of these young people had never written, or even seen a play before, it would have been impossible to give them examples of character *wants* from the canon of dramatic literature. However, they all watched movies and there are ample stories there to draw on. Even very young students understand the concept of a "want," without actually knowing that they do. Today, when I work with fifth to eighth graders, I use *The Little Mermaid* as a springboard for the discussion of story. When I ask the class what it is that the main character, Ariel, wants, every child in the room can tell me that the answer is "to live on land."

I had already pushed past the edge of the envelope with some of the communication-phobics in class, so I reassured them all that these beginning dialogues needn't exceed one single page. (I have found that most people are countersuggestive as toddlers; almost everyone in the group exceeded this limitation.) I also assured them that no one would have to read their dialogues aloud next time. This clearly provided some relief. There were only two people absent from the next class, and one of them was legitimately ill. While no one was asked to read their *own* dialogues aloud, I cast them in each other's.

I chose the more verbally confident students to be the first readers, and then bent over backward and forward to address *all* of my comments to the *writers* of the dialogues. This was tricky because some readers *raced*, some were inaudible, and some stumbled over illegible handwriting; however, all of these problems kept giving birth to new and more wonderful opportunities. For one, the students *themselves* decided that future dialogues should be typed, particularly those readers who felt as though they were being perceived poorly. For another, I began to get questions from the writers about how to use grammar correctly; they were frustrated at having their intentions misread. For the first time in these students' lives, they began to make the connection between things such as question marks and the inflection with which something is asked, exclamation points and humor, commas and intelligibility, and so on. It was only class number three, but I knew I was on to something good.

My term *Outlines* began to resemble art history more than English courses. The activities were delineated by the pictures used to generate their writings. I referred to them as Triggers, and each painting was followed by several weeks for revision. Slowly but surely, revising came to be seen as *creative play* rather than tedious homework. I always gave the students one specific problem to solve for each subsequent draft. Rather than seeing these as corrections to make, they seemed to rise to the challenge of finding solutions. The following are some examples of this kind of feedback:

- "She's such an interesting character, how can you keep the grandma on stage longer?"
- "The potential for dramatic tension in the play is terrific. Can you make the husband really beg for forgiveness before the wife says he's forgiven?"
- "Your dialogue is wonderful, but sometimes I lose track of what the characters are responding to. Can you keep everyone's speeches to no longer than one line?"

By carefully observing the students' responses to *my comments,* I noticed they were able to hear my feedback best if I prefaced it with an acknowledgment of what was already working. This is how I came to adopt one of my first teacher–student rules of etiquette. Like two actors in an improvisation, whatever is offered must be accepted with a *yes* first, then modifications can follow. I've found that students, particularly those with communication disorders, must *feel* somewhat successful in order to take the risk of learning more. Over the years that I've supervised other teachers learning to teach this methodology, I've been struck by their inability to say *anything* positive. They feared sounding "like they were lying." These teachers had to be retaught to look for, and acknowledge, the *small victories* within the big challenges.

By midterm all of my students had become used to writing, speaking, and analyzing words. They all had come to know each other's names and respect each other's risk-taking efforts—they were communicating. This is largely because they knew that they were in a safe learning environment, one in which they could count on being taken seriously. The tougher part was getting them to take *themselves* seriously, particularly those who had been getting by on *attitude* for years. I had a mighty struggle with their demons. I talked with these students frankly and fought for what *they* had to say. Eventually they began to take steps outside of their invented public personas. They even began to be recognized for having particular *styles*—minimalist, poetic, aggressive, funny, offbeat, and so on. I gave some of them copies of published plays by writers who had similar stylistic traits. They were so flattered that, lo and behold, they read them, *and* liked them. These excellent examples also reinforced their growing knowledge of grammar and clarity, as well as the proper format and Presentation for a play script. (The material suggested in Appendix I will give you ample exposure to this genre.)

As students began to see themselves as writers, my next *big* discovery emerged: They were not only enjoying writing, they were getting good at it. By the end of the semester, they had each written, and many times re-written, a short play. These plays all had the following:

- A beginning, a middle, and an end
- Two multidimensional characters
- Conflict and resolution
- Some degree of *flow*

The students all had learned a great deal about writing despite the fact that they'd never cracked a textbook. They had not only put their thoughts on paper, they had endured hearing them read publicly each week, and no one had died! The writers survived because they were so focused on solving one *specific problem* each time. This was crucial because I didn't want to overwhelm them with too much feedback at once. The readers had survived because it was someone else's words on the line.

I decided that, like all hardworking playwrights, these young artists deserved a professional Reading. I gathered some of my actor friends and scheduled a *Presentation* of each student's strongest piece for the last day of the term. Some of them actually asked if they could invite family members—they were really going public. I was to read any necessary stage directions. After a brief Rehearsal to discuss the characters' wants in each piece, and the playwrights' intentions, the actors gave themselves over to the importance that these works held for the new writers. I have to confess that I was *blown away* by what ensued.

Coupled with the basic healthy skeleton of these short works, the depth that seasoned actors brought to the plays created a genuinely impressive afternoon of theatre. No one could believe that these were first efforts; and the students were unspeakably honored that working actors had lent their talents to their nascent efforts. While some students certainly had worked harder than others, and consequently came farther, other students simply had farther to go from the start. Some wrote longer pieces, and some developed better presentational habits, but *none* were failures. It may have been the first time in history, when a reading of twenty-eight new plays concluded, that it was the *Audience* who got up and bowed!

This became the basic template for my course over the next few terms, and both the course and the term-end Presentations began to attract a bit of a following. The next year I was asked if I would consider including acting Training, and then piloting it as a double-credit course. It was hoped that this additional Coaching might further address the speech and reading-comprehension problems of previously underachieving students. It seemed like a rather tall order to fill; it had been challenging enough to get them writing well. Additionally, many of them were extremely nonverbal. I agreed to give it a try because ultimately good acting requires the exact same *authenticity* as good writing; I anticipated how well the two studies would compliment one another. I also made a bet with myself that if someone as voiceless as I had once been could act, then anyone could. We set the class limit at fifteen students. I planned to meet with them twice each week—once for an acting class and once for a writing Workshop.

My gamble paid off. Looking back, and having since Coached and directed many actors with multiple Broadway credits, I can tell you that it is actually a lot easier to Coach people who have no bad habits and no preconceived notions about acting. And, because the style of acting that I espouse is one that focuses *on the listener,* not the speaker, it proved to be a powerful antidote to shyness, stuttering, lack of focus, and the whole host of antisocial behaviors that can make people impossible to teach. In the acting class, after meeting the students and spending some time speaking with each one, I selected short published *Monologues* that were appropriate for their respective personas (see the recommended material listed in Appendix I). Initially, we just talked about the characters, and their situations, extensively in class. Then, I encouraged the students to memorize the material by simply reading it over and over, letting their brains photograph the material.

At the next session they each attempted to speak the words they'd memorized while acting on their characters' intentions. They did so with the knowledge that someone in the group was holding their scripts for them. If they *blanked out,* they simply had to say "line" and they would be given the words they needed. There was no penalty for forgetting, and no restriction on the number of times they could call for a *line.* I have found that reciting material from memory is one of the most *stressful forms of public speaking,* and one that teachers regularly call on their students to perform. This can be downright *excruciating* for someone with a communication disorder. Many of the teachers I train quickly discover this when asked to get up and do the same. Some only remember a single line or two their first time, and that is fine. We can still identify the character's want, as well as their own distracting physical habits, in those first few lines.

I sent everyone up with a partner to serve as their listener—the character they were supposed to be talking to in the play. I then emphasized connection, connection, *connection* as they fought for what that character wanted. Their partner served as a buddy in the *ocean of fear* that is public speaking and the intense focus on them was their lifeline. In the end, this directive to connect was tremendously effective, but it took weeks to get some communication-phobics to make either eye or physical contact. They found every possible way to hide: staring at the floor, pulling their hair in front of their faces, turning their backs to the class, forgetting their words, and/or becoming inaudible. In turn, I scrutinized them more and more closely. I lovingly provided kudos for any *little* thing they were able to accomplish: remembering even one line, looking up even once, or making sense of the material. I used this kind of *fear management* to allow them to experience "being seen" as a *positive* thing—maybe for the first time in some of their lives. Over the weeks, I encouraged students to do each of these little things a little more. They slowly grew from being painful to watch, to becoming committed and focused communicators.

I began every Coaching session by asking each student what the character they were portraying wanted. The benefits of that question were twofold. As it turned out, Monologue study was a de facto reading-comprehension assessment tool. It was impossible for them to fight for what their characters wanted unless they *knew* what that *want* was. Additionally, keeping them focused on that *positive want* proved, for some, to be the way out of their own depressed states. For example, in a scene involving a romantic breakup, the *negative want* would be stated as "I *don't want* her to leave me"; I requested that the positive want be stated as, "I *want* her to stay."

Almost all students are afraid to show their anger because people are encouraged all of their lives to calm down, lower their voice, be nice, and not to talk back. But most are stuck in negativity. With teens and adults, especially females, I have to spend an enormous amount of time and energy inviting them to fight for what they want. I explain over and over again the *difference* between *fighting with* and *fighting for*, but many still view anger as an exclusively negative emotion. Even when they come to believe that anger can be a life-affirming force, they still can't abide expressing it. I have to coax the *fight* out of my students. I do so by making their listener as uncooperative as possible. I have them turning away, getting up to leave, even refusing to listen. This forces the speaker to physically demand a response. When that *determined* sensation is experienced, I begin to see an entirely different human being emerge.

It was once explained to me that depression isn't sadness, but anger being held in. Like holding a ball down under the water, holding it in drains a lot of energy. When some of the depressive students allowed themselves to become *energetic in fighting for* what their characters wanted, they suddenly *became audible*. And, when they really became *engaged with the listener* whom they wanted something from, they suddenly *became sociable*. There is *nothing more transformative* than believing that there are things in life worth fighting for, and that they can be won. The transformations were palpable to everyone in the room. Some of the least promising students were the stars at the term-end Presentations of each other's plays. To reduce time and stress, these plays were presented as Rehearsed Readings rather than memorized performances. But the students had learned to be so committed to each other, and to their material, that the Audience soon forgot that there were scripts in hand. Once again, I marveled at how far students could come in a single term and was pleased to learn that more than a few of them went on to declare English as their majors.

So, the Find Your Voice™ methodology was born. Soon after, we were unable to seat all of the guests who wanted to attend the final Presentations. One semester I had a student who taught at the Children's Aid Society, which was around the corner on Sullivan Street. She brought the Center's directors to see the work. Afterward, they informed me that there was a large unused theatre space at their

Center which could be used for future Presentations. It was offered free of charge with one caveat—bring my methodology to their after-school program for teenagers. I had never intended to teach writing in the first place, nor had I planned to teach acting to college students who had no background in theatre. I simply had to play out the hand that fate was dealing me. Six months later I was sitting in *the circle*, surrounded by students no older than I was when I had learned to love school for the first time.

So many of these young people turned out to be mirrors of the teen I had been. Some possessed talent in singing or writing, but all were locked away from their own authentic voices. Without being totally aware of it, I endeavored to recreate the environment I had come to life in. Over the next ten years I honed the Find Your Voice™ methodology, which I had developed quite by accident in a college classroom. I did so without ever diluting the rigor, or diminishing the standards, for this younger age group. And once in a more flexible venue, I even incorporated some vocal and movement training. I essentially created a Find Your Voice™ conservatory where I could integrate and apply all that I had mastered in the search for *my voice*. Then I set out to fill this conservatory with students who reflected the true colors of the city, in every way.

Under the name of the Sullivan Street Players, I taught about fifty teens per year. I also tried to maintain an ethnic, socioeconomic, and academic balance in the membership each term. This included students from some of the most challenged schools and neighborhoods in the city, as well as some of the most advantaged. The majority of the students came to me through social service or educational feeder groups. The *common denominator* was always their *desire* to find their voices. Because the focus was exclusively on the work we were there to do, everything else took care of itself. There is no greater way to break down cultural and intellectual barriers than through *inter-acting*. Partners in a scene not only come to establish a level of intimacy through their characters, but they also become absolutely dependent on one another during the performance. Scenes are not successful unless *both* actors are engaged.

Ironically, it was often the less academically successful students who wrote the more creative plays. Similarly, many of these students also had greater access to their own imaginations as actors than those who had learned well how to spit back information on an exam. This level playing field required constant caretaking however, and was sustained only through relationship-based teaching. I've worked with failing students who had no adult at home for them, students who had been on Ritalin for years, and brilliant and talented students with no social skills at all (see Chapter Six, *Profiles of Courage*). Each and every student possessed their own communication demons; what was easy for one was almost impossible for another. However, they were all led to the point where they could honor each other's struggles and victories. This was directly attributable to the fact that they all witnessed the authentic interactions between me and each of the other students in the circle. On many occasions they watched each other overcome their own greatest personal communication obstacles. Some finally became audible, some got through a speech without stuttering, some made physical contact with another person for the first time, and so on. Following these breakthroughs it was not uncommon for the rest of the members of the circle to spontaneously break into applause, or even tears.

Over the next decade, I continued to fine-tune my inner-city conservatory. I accepted *any* New York City teenager who was willing to make the commitment to *attending* each week *and* to *doing* all of the homework involved in memorizing and re-writing material. They all studied at the college level, and they were all expected to behave like professionals. I continued to use visual Triggers as the point of departure for the writing, but also began to incorporate the use of social themes, music, and dance as the stimuli. Because these teen companies always consisted of about twenty-five very diverse members, the various responses to the Triggers became an artistic genre of its own—I called it *Clustering*. A *Cluster* is essentially a group of thematically linked plays, much like a collection of related short stories or a cycle of poems. Because the young writers *were so diverse,* so too were their styles of expression. However, there were always some echoes from piece to piece. Identifying the echoes became a source of delight at question-and-answer (Q&A) sessions that followed each public Presentation, with their similarly diverse Audience members. These Q&As also offered another opportunity for the new voices to be heard (see Chapter Five, *Ending on a High Note: Going Public*).

There were other wonderful benefits of the *Cluster approach*—for one, the ample and substantive roles for all of the Company members. Unlike a full-length play in which there might be only three or four meaty roles, these short plays were all limited to two characters (see Chapter Four, *The Methodology: Writing and Re-Writing*). Another benefit was that the discipline required to tell a story with any depth in only five to ten pages proved to be the greatest focusing exercise of all. Anyone can ramble on, but only a craftsperson can hone a piece to be clear, concise, and affecting. It was not the writing but the *re-writing* that made these short plays into works of art. The final Presentations themselves were then produced, with the highest professional *production values*, to honor the efforts of the young artists. Set, light, and costume designers all brought their talents to the mix. I was directing a great deal at this time in my life, and I personally enjoyed this layer of the process; it was very exciting for the students too. However, I want to stress that all of it was not *essential*. What was essential was that the *process* was of excellence, and that the students had the *opportunity* to go public. That can be accomplished very nicely with a simple Rehearsed Reading before an invited Audience, which is how all of my shorter Trainings culminate now (again, see Chapter Five).

What was also essential was the quality of the re-acting and re-writing itself. The work of the Sullivan Street Players was so authentic, and of such a high artistic caliber, that we began to be sought out for collaborations with other organizations—including Phoenix House, the Children of Alcoholics Foundation, and three New York City museums (see Chapter Six, *Profiles of Courage: Teens*). Part of the power of the work was that young people were speaking to other young people in their own voices. Part of the power was that they said what they had to say with craft. Initially, the Cluster pieces ran long—up to twelve short plays were included. But the Audiences, both young and old, watched with rapt attention. The teachers who brought classes to matinees often warned me that the kids would *never sit still* for a serious drama running upward of two hours; they did, and then they stayed to participate in the Q&A session!

At that time, there were very few programs like this for New York City teens. This was an opportunity for young people, whose communication skills were not particularly strong, to find and hone their voices. Now, twenty years later, there is a proliferation of programs where anyone can be led to presenting their original works. More and more, there is pressure on teachers, particularly English teachers, to do the same during the schoolday. It is indeed wonderful to see that this approach has become a *movement*—one that had never included the voiceless. However, when it is done well, it is highly delicate work at best. I've often felt like a labor coach as I brought a new voice into the world. When it is not done well, presenting reluctant communicators can either demean the participants or the art. That was the impetus for me to write this book. I wanted to share what I have learned in order to reach a greater number of people with communication disorders.

After ten years at the Children's Aid Society, Find Your Voice™ became a respected, citywide approach to literacy improvement and art-making. Although my goal was human development rather than professional development, some real talent also emerged from these previously untrained students; some went on to Juilliard, Broadway, and Hollywood. Our performances were regularly attended by *general* Audiences of both adults and teens. The unintended outcomes highlight my belief that, even with poor communicators, if the focus remains on the development of craft, the sky is the limit. In addition to receiving numerous commissions and awards, we even attracted a respectable Advisory Board and an independent funding stream. The gift that I had hoped to give back was being received by hundreds of students.

It was time to "marry" this educational work to my long-standing goal of creating a professional company in which to keep my voice strong. In 1994, I established Starfish Theatreworks—a nonprofit Company dedicated to bringing unheard voices into the world. I went on to develop and produce some twenty new professional works for the Main stage during our first seven years. Simultaneously, our educational program brought the Find Your Voice™ methodology to another couple of hundred young people. Many former students now teach, make art, and administer Starfish as professionals alongside of me.

Over the years we have offered many matinee performances of teen work for hundreds of school Audiences. More and more, I began to be sought out by in- and after-school teachers who also wanted their students to develop and present original material. They hoped to improve students' abilities to articulate themselves and wanted to learn my methodology. This is what led to the development of the Teacher Training initiative; it began as a pilot for English teachers, then grew to include teachers of every subject who wanted to help *all* students become more articulate.

Because I have always been a believer in *experiential learning,* I decided the best way to transfer the skill was to ask teachers to undertake the same journey the teens had. They would move from free-write; to re-write; to public Presentation. In doing so, they would have the opportunity to first grapple with their own communication disorders, which were manifold. I heard all of the same defenses and excuses about why they hadn't memorized their Monologues, or rewritten their plays, as I had always heard from teenage students. Despite the fact that these teachers stood in front of a classroom all day, *most were terribly afraid* of public speaking. They were also *terrified of* the potential for *negative judgment* that was involved in sharing their writing. So many teachers, even English teachers, have issues about memorizing material or seeing a piece of writing through to completion. Some are so afraid that they try to withdraw from participating the night before a Workshop is due to begin. The greatest transformation teachers undergo during the Trainings is not the acquisition of a basic re-acting and re-writing craft, but the acquisition of *empathy* for their students. Sadly, this seems to be a term that is too rarely seen in teacher training texts.

I asked the teachers to *re-experience the terror* of being called on to read private writing aloud, to speak memorized words in front of a group, and to face the broader judgment of a public Audience. In the process, these teachers began to understand just how difficult it is for a noncommunicative young person to be called on simply to answer a question in class. They also experienced what it feels like to be *Coached*—they liked the feeling. Much of my effort went into gaining their trust and making it safe for them to take risks; the task of skill acquisition paled in comparison. They also bridled against, and then eventually embraced, the high standards that were set for them in terms of attendance, punctuality, preparedness, concentration, connectedness, and graciousness. I've found that veteran teachers, in particular, struggle when they have to be new learners again. But when they were treated as a Company of professionals, many of them felt that way for the first time in a long time; as with the teens, real talent always emerged (see Chapter Seven, *More Profiles of Courage: Teachers*).

And as with the teens, the focus of the Trainings was always on the work—pedagogy was never discussed per se. The teachers simply *did* what they wanted their students to do, then they *felt and saw* from me what their students needed to feel from a Coach. Like the teens again, I never encountered a teacher who didn't find the authenticity of their own voices by the end of even a three-week Workshop. Now, thousands of young people are being taught in this manner by the teachers who found their voices through this methodology. These teachers work in settings that range from elementary schools to colleges, from in-school to after-school, from conservatory to tutorial, from English-speaking to Spanish-speaking, from alternative to conventional. While most don't yet have the depth of knowledge that I do after so many years of study and practice, they have all learned what is most crucial for finding a voice. They have learned to establish a trusting relationship, to set high standards, and to help their students to connect and to pursue positive wants.

In the summer of 2002, the National Endowment for the Arts funded a pilot to observe the *turnkey teaching* of this methodology. I devised a model in which I would supervise ten teachers, who had previously trained with me, while they taught the Find Your Voice™ methodology to a Company of summer school students. The course was only three weeks long and met for three hours each day. Most of the participating teachers had studied with me for less than a total of twenty-five hours. Although I had received countless written and verbal testimonials about their teaching transformations over the years, the purpose of the pilot was to see how well these teachers could *implement* their new skills. They could, but I was amazed by their lack of belief in their own ability to do so. Although they rallied by the end of the pilot, the teachers second-guessed themselves constantly during the first week. In addition, because they were anxious, they became more the teachers they had been and less the Coaches they had hoped to become.

Old teaching habits are indeed difficult to break, and it is even more difficult if the learner has never been the *recipient* of relationship-based teaching. I suppose it's akin to expecting someone who was poorly parented to be a good parent. Although entering into this kind of *learning relationship* is ultimately mutually satisfying for both the teacher and the students, I don't begin to imagine that after simply reading this book a teacher will teach differently ever after. It will require practice, trust, and possibly participation in one or more of my Workshops. (For more on Find Your Voice™ Workshops, visit www.Starfishtheatreworks.com.) Becoming aware of a communication problem, however, is the first step toward solving it.

While this first chapter has emphasized the development of my educational methodology, the remaining chapters focus more on acquiring the craft that is both the vehicle and the end product. If possessing a map leads one toward a solution, then I invite you to get out your compass and start the journey.

2 The Learning Environment: Orientation

I believe that the success of finding voices depends, to a great extent, on the success of the first time(s) the class meets as a Company. Experience shows that the ultimate level of trust and sharing is strongest if it's established right at the beginning. This is when the terror, in the form of fear of the unknown, is at its greatest. Similarly, the fulfillment of the entire journey very much depends on the success of the ending. This is when the participants go *public*, either in a Rehearsed Reading or a fully produced Presentation (see Chapter Five, *Ending on a High Note: Going Public*).

Whether you plan to use this methodology in an academic classroom, or in an after-school setting, I strongly suggest beginning with an *Orientation*, which provides exactly what the word implies: a time for the participants to get used to a new environment and a new set of ideas. My after-school Orientations typically consist of one three-hour session. But, the same approach has been successfully adapted to a school-day framework by dividing the recommended Orientation activities into three or four shorter sessions. The Orientation's goals are to help participants feel:

1. Safe (trusting of the teacher)—weave the net
2. Professional (capable of the level of skills they will receive)—set the tone

3. Connected (to one another)—build the team
4. Excited (about the work)—build commitments

Weaving the Net—Trust-Building

Throughout this book, I emphasize that fear management seems to be key to any pursuit involving public sharing. During Orientation, when everyone and everything is new, public sharing is as basic as having to speak your name before the group. This is why the teacher must begin to manage fear from the moment the participants walk through the door. I'm sure that many of you reading this book would never take a Workshop if you thought you'd be called on to perform before a group in any way. That is precisely what public sharing is, and what teachers regularly ask of students.

For this reason, I greet every participant with a reassuring smile, and I look into their eyes. Then by name, if I know it, I welcome and invite them in. As obvious as this may sound, I have found that, after kindergarten, most teachers don't do it. This simple gesture of acknowledgment telegraphs to students that their experience with me is going to be relationship-based. The intention behind this approach is not to be nice, but to be *present*. It is a torturous and vulnerable thing to sit anonymously in a chair waiting for something involving you, but unknown to you, to begin. If teachers can in any way alleviate the distress, I believe that they will already be on their way to winning the trust of their students. And *trust* is the *prerequisite* to articulation.

When the class does begin, I have the students take their seats within a circle of chairs; then I perform another basic, but often forgotten, ritual—I close the door. Again this sounds obvious, but I have visited so many public school classrooms where the voices out in the hallway were far stronger than any the teacher could hope to cultivate inside the room that term. I know that keeping the doors open is the policy at some schools, but it is worth petitioning the principal for a waiver. It is absolutely crucial that an environment conducive to listening be established right from the beginning, which gives participants confidence that their risk-taking will be *contained*. I make sure this containment is vigilantly maintained throughout each and every session.

Some of the teachers that I've observed, after their Training with me, have misapplied containment as punitive discipline by ordering their students to "sit still, and quietly." I like to view it as inviting them to the party. Many times during every acting session, I look to the group to affirm the transformations that another student is making as he or she works. I also ask particular individuals if they can recognize their own struggles while watching someone else's. As the group develops ownership of their craft, they even come to anticipate the feedback that I'm going to offer their colleagues. In fact, some of the most satisfying moments of the term have been when participants shared a collective moment of awe. Often, this occurs when they witness someone accomplishing something that was previously impossible. In short, experience shows that students will learn to communicate best if they also *participate as keen observers.* I explain it to them this way. Toward that end, I cultivate their ability to commit by maximizing their ability to concentrate—by maintaining a *listening environment.* Plus, until students are ready to go public, closing the door ensures that what they say and do remains private.

Once everyone is quiet and focused, and headphones and coats have been reluctantly removed, I begin by explaining that they are now members of a new Company. This Company has been brought together for the common pursuit of finding voices. In that pursuit they will all learn to communicate original, well-crafted ideas, with the intention of generating a constructive response. They will accomplish this by developing their skills in speaking, reading, writing, and listening. Each member will address his or her personal limitations, at his or her own pace.

I also explain that I will be there to guide them through this experience, and that I know how scary communicating can be. I tell them a little about my background; and the challenges of writing, directing, and teaching. I reiterate again and again that I will be their ally in the process, and that I will help them to be successful. I assure them too that, while I will give them the tools they need to trust seeing and being seen, they will learn much from watching one another: "This is why our classroom must be a place where people can concentrate, take risks, and be vulnerable to each other. This is also the reason why we will uphold an unalterable *Golden Rule:* No one may laugh at anyone's attempt to communicate—ever."

While sharing this information, I try to make eye contact with each student. I slowly scan the circle while I speak in a warm professional tone that is neither patronizing nor intimidating. Over the years of training other teachers, I have often received positive feedback about the tone of my voice—calm, straightforward, and connected. Whether I was saying something complimentary or something difficult to hear, they felt it was one of the most "embracing" things they'd ever experienced. It seems that when teachers are only present from the neck up, the room is filled with their ideas but not with their hearts and souls; their more complete selves are somewhere outside of the room. Students, sensing this incompleteness, follow them out the door. If one is going to teach people to communicate and connect effectively, the skill must be modeled at all times.

Throughout this initial talk, I continually stop to ask for questions and comments. I remind students that this is *their* learning time, and I encourage them to actively take ownership of it. Even if they can't rise to this kind of participation during the first week, the constant invitation to do so seems to work its magic down the road.

Setting the Tone—Skill-Building

The ultimate goal of this Training is improved communication skills; the proof of which will be in a final act of public sharing. I view each group of students as a professional Company *preparing to perform* together, and I view the classroom as their conscrvatory. As such, I abide by many of the traditions and expectations afforded any Company of professionals.

THE CONTACT SHEET

We begin by circulating a *Contact Sheet*—a list of the participants and how they can be contacted: telephone/beeper numbers, email and street addresses, and so on. Having a list of each other's names is crucial; it hastens the process by which they all become familiar with one another. I provide this even if my students already know each other, because one of my goals is to have them *get to know each other in a new way*. The contact information is also important, both to enable scene partners to get together for some outside rehearsing and to foster interaction between the members. I know that this sharing of private data can be dicey in a public school setting; however, when I've spent the extra time to get parental permission to do so, it's been well worth the effort. If it's not possible to share contact information, I still create a roster of participants' names. I ask students to make sure that their information is accurate, jotting down correct spellings, and numbers when authorized during the session. I also let them know that new sheets will be circulated at the next meeting; if I'm going to demand revision, I'd better be willing to offer it!

THE MANUAL

In addition to the Contact Sheet, I distribute and briefly review a Find Your Voice™ Manual*; the binder should contain the following.

A Letter of Welcome. ■ This should be something personal, and in the teacher's own voice. It should describe the expectations for the Company, including a statement of the importance of punctuality and regular attendance. This is crucial because the *work is experiential* and cannot be made up by simply reviewing someone else's notes. Also, the Workshop process is only effective if there is a sufficient number of participants to serve as respondents and partners. After hearing this letter, each student should understand that their role in the class is crucial to everyone's success, and that *no one* will remain invisible or anonymous.

After reading the letter aloud, I describe how this approach might be a little different from other classes they've taken. Here they will be practicing the skills they're being taught during each session; and they will be continually sharing and responding to each other's work, which is also why they are seated in a circle. (When this kind of formation is simply impossible, because desks have to remain in rows or clusters, teachers can ask the students to turn their chairs toward the center of the room so that they can at least see each other better.) The circle also allows them to watch me work with other members of the class, although there will be no sense of competition.

Each student will be grappling with the things that they personally find difficult. There will also be *no tests* per se because with my help they will be demonstrating their growing craft every time we meet. I then explain to students that the class may also seem different to them in that I don't ever want them to do anything I say, *unless they understand* the purpose of the direction. In fact if they do simply comply, they will not be learning to communicate effectively on their own. *Creation of dialogue* is the goal at every level.

Some Information About What Re-Acting *Is.* ■ If most of the students in the group have never had any acting training, the mere mention of this word will be enough to cause a tidal wave of anxiety in the room. The Manual should offer a full discussion about *re-acting*. If you still don't have a fairly clear idea of what it is after reading this book, please read it again—and again—before you attempt to teach the process. (Or take one of my Trainings.) At the

---

**If you, or your school, wish to purchase a sample Find Your Voice™ Manual, contact: STWorks2@aol.com. For Training see www.starfishtheatreworks.com.*

Orientation, I share four basic and reassuring truths about this methodology:

- The Training focuses on *doing, not on feeling.* Students will not be told to cry, scream, or relive their childhood traumas. They are simply to pursue the actions that would be appropriate if they were in the same situation as the character in a play they've been assigned to study.
- Everyone will be *nervous and self-conscious* at first, but all of their attention ultimately should be focused on the person they want something from. Students always work in pairs, so that they can become *"other-conscious."*
- It is often the *shyest* students who *become* the most *powerful re-actors* by the end of the study.
- The Coach will never require them to do anything, *without first helping* them find the courage to try it.

By the end of the term—believe it or not—students are so engaged in what they're doing together that they practically forget that anyone is in the Audience watching. They even enjoy it. To reinforce this notion, I tell them: "Almost everyone gets nervous when they speak or perform in front of other people—even famous movie and rock stars. In fact, public speaking is the number one fear in the world." My goal is to *enable them to speak* out despite the fact that it's scary. I am not necessarily interested in grooming students to become career performers, just to become empowered people. They can all become confident to raise their hands in any class, and become future professionals who can proudly share their ideas in any field.

Guidelines for Writing a Good Short Play. ■ Again, you should have some notion about what would be a good approach—and why—after reading this book. If not, you don't have enough ownership of the craft to proceed (review Chapter Four).

A Short Sample Play. ■ To demonstrate the proper manuscript format, and to inspire, include an actual play. Many collections of short plays are available locally; or you can write me for permission to use a Find Your Voice™ teen-written play. After you've found a few voices yourself, include the best of your own students' work here.

A Glossary. ■ Include the list that will be used during the Training. I suggest that the glossary only contain those terms that you feel comfortable with, fully grasp, and will really use.

This binder becomes the student's handbook for the term. All of their acting assignments, as well as the multiple drafts of their plays, can be brought to each class in it. With younger students the Manuals can be left in the classroom, as long as whatever they need to work on goes home. In addition to serving as an important resource, the binder serves as a reminder to the participants that they are now in a Company; this Manual is proof of their common membership. I have met many former teenage and teacher students who still owned and used their Manuals many years after initial Trainings.

THE SCHEDULE

Next, I circulate a *Schedule*, which indicates what will be covered at each session and on what dates the term-end Presentations will occur. In the after-school format, following Orientation, half of each weekly three-hour session is devoted to re-acting and half to re-writing. I like to do both at every session because the study of each one so greatly informs the other. A minimum of about twenty-five to thirty hours is needed to complete the entire journey from Orientation to final Presentation. This journey has been equally successful as a stand-alone, six-week program or within a schoolday context. For instance, it has been implemented during three or four weekly writing Workshops, English, or global studies classes. Often the Trigger that was selected related to a current topic of study. It also worked fine when spread out over a time frame that was as long as two ten-week after-school terms, or during schoolday Advisory Groups that meet once a week. Additional time simply allows members to study more than one Monologue or scene, and the Trainings can culminate in a fuller Presentation. It has also been run in the summer during three intensive weeks with daily meetings. In that case, group members studied only one piece, and the Training culminated in a Rehearsed Reading.

In every case, there were unavoidable disruptions in such things as student attendance and space availability, as well as unforeseen obstacles. Although it never seemed like it would, the journey always came together in the end if the "map"—Schedule—was well prepared in the beginning. As the two sample Schedule options in Appendix II indicate, it is not the time frame but the *sequence of activities* that is *crucial*. I find that having a Schedule not only helps to orient the students as to what they can expect, but it also begins to give them some ownership of the process. During my own education, I always found that those teachers whose style was less relationship-based favored the element of surprise—knowledge was their power. As far as I'm concerned, if you want to inculcate a skill that requires trust, your advantage is greater if learners *carry as little anticipatory anxiety as possible*—knowledge is student power!

Make sure students are privy to the number of drafts they will be expected to write, and when the final *Polish* will be due. (Once the Treatment for their play is approved, students usually prepare four drafts plus a *Polish*, with additional re-writes required during Table-Work). They also need to know how many Showings of each scene or Monologue assignment they will be doing, and for which of those they will be expected to have memorized the material. (Students usually present three memorized Showings after their first Read Through. Each Showing should demonstrate increasing flow, with the piece ultimately being performed from memory.) In my experience, students have been most successful when the *journey* toward their own voices was *laid out in knowable and manageable steps.* This required advanced planning on my part, as well as courage on theirs.

Getting Connected—Team-Building

Once what we're here to do together is established, and we know what the rules of the game are, we can begin to play. Although I'm not a believer in the need for theatre games per se, I do believe that re-actors must prepare their bodies and voices by *warming up.* At this point, particularly if the Orientation is being conducted in one long session, I usually get the students on their feet. First, I say that we're going to do a few simple stretches and vocalizations, as a group. No formal dance or voice training is required to learn (or to teach) any of these exercises. I also explain that this will give me the opportunity to point out a few things about their *physical* instruments and to observe what they are each comfortable doing. No one will be graded or judged in any way; it is simply a way for all of us to begin *learning and relaxing together.* Stretches can be done at the beginning of each session.

Anything that involves the use of the body, especially with teenagers, will engender anxiety. I try to name the anxiety before the activity is undermined by giggling, or other acting out: "I know that this may feel odd at first, even silly, because most of your day is devoted to thinking and not to doing. But the voice is generated in the body not the mind, and that is where we have to find it. Everyone is self-conscious right now, but being more conscious of your physical self is exactly the place to start."

Once the class is up and in a circle, I begin by asking them to stand with their weight evenly distributed on both feet. This seemingly minor physical adjustment, once made, can have major physical and attitudinal ramifications for the students. Many people, particularly teenage girls, stand primarily on one foot with their body weight sunken into one hip. This not only projects an aura of boredom, it lulls the body into a state of passivity. When the weight is on both feet, evenly distributed from heel to toes and aligned with the hips and shoulders to provide a broad base of support, the student is ready to spring—ready to act. Later on in the term, all I have to do is glance at my students' feet and they automatically make this adjustment, usually, with a smile on their faces that reflects the pride of having anticipated me.

I then ask students to make sure that their bodies are facing out, and that they are open to *giving and receiving* information. Their chins should be up, their eyes off of the floor and focused, their hands unclenched, and their diaphragms uncrunched. This *open position* will begin to teach their bodies the kind of receptivity *necessary for communicating*. Before moving on, I take the time to observe each participant, giving those who are ready a nod. I gently invite the others to come further out by modeling a specific adjustment. An example might be: "You look terrific, now just lift your eyes so that we can really see each other." If you haven't explored your own skeletal flexibility in years, try to do so, or you will not be a positive model. (A stretch-and-tone class at a local Y could be very helpful.)

EXERCISES TO OPEN THE BODY

Once the group is fully awake and "present," you can do some of the following additional exercises if you are comfortable leading them. Have everyone do one or more of these as time allows.

- Roll slowly over—bend—leading with the head and fingertips, reaching for the toes; this will decompress the spine. Roll only as far as you can go without straining the back in any way; hold. Roll up slowly with the head rising last; repeat.
- While standing upright, bend and roll the head in slow circles from right to left and back again; this works out the tension in the neck.
- Open the eyes wide and roll the eyeballs slowly in circles from left, to ceiling, to right, to the floor, and back again; this strengthens muscles in the visual receptors.

- Squeeze the hands into tight fists, hold, and then slowly open with fully extended fingers; this releases tension in the tactile receptors.
- Raise the shoulders slowly to the ears, hold, and slowly release; this eases tension in the shoulders. Repeat.

The next three exercises can, and should, be done by everyone.

- Slowly open the jaw as wide as possible, as if you're going to bite into a pumpkin; this works out tension in the face, and begins an exploration of the cavity that contains and releases the voice. Hold, slowly close, and then repeat. Because the mouth is the source of the literal voice, just opening it wide will be distressing for a lot of students. Many even think it's open wide when it's barely open at all. Those who are struggling should put their fingers against the outside of their cheeks, press lightly between their upper and lower molars, and try again with their fingers in that position. Some students will not be able to open their mouths very wide for weeks. I tell them it will take time to release all of the tension that has accumulated; then I remind myself that this tension is exactly why they're here.
- Take a slow breath in through the nose and then release it slowly through the mouth, as if you're blowing out a candle. After four times, open the mouth wider to release the breath with an "ah" sound—like a sigh. Repeat, producing even more sound the second time.
- Breathe in slowly through the nose, with jaws open pumpkinstyle. On that same "ah" sound, release the breath and sustain it on any comfortable pitch. Because almost everyone gets itchy about singing, I put the focus only on staying together as a group. I don't conduct; I ask the group to listen to and to watch each other. They should breathe in together, release and say "ah" on the *same pitch together*, and get off of the note to find silence together. Some will race to be the first to do everything; others will trail behind, or attempt to be the loudest. There can be no individual winners. If the sound doesn't seem like one seamless voice, everyone loses. This will be the first *group effort*, and it will probably have to be repeated many times before it can be done successfully.

This simple act of intense group watching and listening will go a long way toward breaking down some of the invisible barriers between the participants. Now they are ready to share a little more personally. At this point I ask the group to sit so that we can go around the circle and share names. We don't share the names their parents gave to them, we share names that they would like to give to themselves. As always, I assure them that there are no wrong answers. I explain that the stakes are pretty low—they won't ever be addressed by these names.

THE NAME GAME

Because the goal of this methodology is to encourage public sharing by improving self-esteem, I begin the Training by inviting the students to be seen in the way that they would like to be seen. I have them highlight an authentic attribute about themselves of which they are very proud. This is done through the choice of a descriptive Native American style name. The choice is difficult for many students, for many reasons. I have found that people with communication disorders often don't want anyone to know anything about them at all, they expect to have any expression of themselves ridiculed, and/or they can't think of anything about which they feel proud.

Again, I try to *name* their potential reaction to the exercise before they can even have it: "We all worry about the way other people might react to us. We might be tempted to say something goofy, or not to answer at all. It will take courage, but try to assume that you'll get a positive response; that's what we're all here to learn how to do. Everyone's in the same boat." Not unlike the Dramaturgical Inter-Play that will soon follow their free-writing, this exercise requires vigilant listening, and much encouragement on the part of the teacher.

I explain that they should attach the new name to their old first name. Then, after emphatically envoking the Golden Rule, I always go first. I try to offer an example that is both honest and reassuring: "I'm Gail-Listens-with-Her-Eyes." As we go around in the circle, many of the students play by the rules, particularly after they see me rewarding those who did so before them. Others, especially the boys, are often too embarrassed to say anything authentic. They either make fun of themselves or of the exercise. I try to remind myself that this is just a defense, and that it's probably there for good reason. A boy may offer something like: "I'm Jon-Greatest-Guy-in-the-World." I compliment him on his self-love, and then ask if his *want* was for us to see him as conceited or to hold him to that impossibly high standard. Boys will usually just smirk and shrug this kind of question off, but they will have seen that I am going to take them seriously even when they cannot. They will also have learned something about wants.

If the student's response is, "I don't have anything to say," I ask them a nonthreatening question: "What is your favorite color?" or

"When were you born?" Then I dub them "Jasmin-Loves-Yellow" or "Erica-Child-of-Spring." By the end of the circle, and with the pressure off, these previously mute students often ask me for another chance to choose a name for themselves. I always grant it. Not unlike responses to the photographic Triggers, the responses to the Name Game reveal a great deal about the personalities, interests, and fears of the participants. If you listen carefully, they teach you, and each other, much about themselves. Their new names can provide the surest paths to their centers of trust, so I always jot them down beside their real names on my Contact Sheet.

As the term goes along, I often remind students of their choices at a salient moment. One girl dubbed herself "Sherisse-Longs-to-Be-Free." Weeks later, in acting class, she was resisting a direction to let her character really fight for the mother's permission to leave home. I told her that if she found the courage to join the battle onstage, she might stop "longing to be free" offstage! At first she stared at me, not comprehending at all. Then she smiled when she recognized her own words, and her own dilemma. We shared a private moment in the middle of her public sharing. By reexperiencing the proof that I had really heard her that first day, her trust in me grew exponentially.

Generating Excitement—Commitment-Building

By now the participants have all survived a taste of seeing and being seen, from my initial greeting through to the Name Game. Their public sharing can now go deeper. This is when I have them write.

THE FREE-WRITE AND INTER-PLAY

I briefly explain the purpose and parameters of a triggered free-write, then I ask them all to take out a pen and a piece of paper. I always have extras for the unprepared. I begin by placing several copies of a chosen photo at different angles on the floor within the circle. It is best to always choose an image that inspires, not dictates, a story. I have found that *close-up* shots of interesting objects and moody rooms work best; whatever is chosen should be story-full. Some of my past favorites include a broken umbrella lying in the street—who threw it there, and why?; a used tea bag—who was drinking the tea, and who were they with?; a chair in front of a closed door—who was sitting in it, where did they go, and who is behind the door?

I remind students once again that there are no wrong answers; and that, although we will eventually share them aloud, this exercise will neither be graded nor judged. I also free them from worries about grammar and spelling; I encourage them to just think out loud on paper: "Write whatever comes into your heads even if it seems to make no sense at all; just keep the pen moving and don't cross anything out. I will ask you to stop in five minutes." (Younger students, who write more slowly, might need ten minutes.)

I acknowledge that this will be a little awkward for those who are not used to writing their thoughts down on paper. Then, I stress that it's really no different from describing feelings or situations out loud. I also let them know: "It may be tempting to make fun of the exercise by writing something silly, or by not writing anything at all. Those responses are just symptoms of the fear of communicating—that is the fear you are here to conquer." Again, I've found that by naming those reactions in advance, it makes them less attractive. Other than that, silence should prevail.

After I disclose the image, I remind them that there should be no talking to each other about what they see; all of their energy should go into their writing. If I do see someone talking, or not writing anything, I approach her or him and privately ask whether I can help. The social talkers usually clam up; the frozen writers insist that they have "nothing to say." In the latter case, I encourage them to simply describe what they see, and to write down something that it reminds them of. If someone absolutely refuses to write anything—which does happen—I attempt to get a response during the verbal Inter-Play that follows. It's not ideal, nor is it easy, but it usually yields something, which can then be built on. I always try to remember that, for the communicatively disabled, committing anything of themselves to paper is extremely scary.

While the group is writing, I ordinarily use the opportunity to observe and to take in more information about the members. I note these things on my own Contact Sheet while I stand guard over their listening environment. For many students, it is tough to get started so, if they stare at me, I simply telegraph encouragement to them by nodding or smiling. (I urge teachers who haven't written in a long time to do the free-write along with the group. It's difficult not to preconceive a response—since you select the Trigger—so you should begin again with a second idea.)

After four minutes I let the group know that there is only one minute left, and that they should start wrapping it up. I pick up the Trigger image and then ask everyone to put down their pens. At this point, I remind students that we'll now begin going around the circle to share the pieces aloud. This causes another tidal wave of anxiety. I assure them that *everyone is feeling nervous,* and that I'm not at all fazed by that fact. I reiterate many times that I understand how scary this is, that I will treat their writing with the utmost respect, and that I've done it myself many times. (If you haven't shared your writing aloud recently, you should probably read yours aloud as well.)

I try to diffuse the tension with humor too:

> Before you all start asking to go to the restroom, I want to promise you that I am not expecting works of literary genius. I am looking for insights into what you might enjoy writing about. It could be one sentence, or even one word, that opens a window. This will be scary, both because you'll be sharing your thoughts and because everyone will be watching you read. But, we are all in the same boat. Besides, I'm the one that has to help you come up with some great ideas for a play based on these doodles; imagine how much I'm sweating! I realize that you don't really know me yet, and have no reason to trust me yet, but I am determined to earn your trust.

I also explain that at first some students write long and other students write short, but *all* wind up with a play by the end of the term. Lastly, I reassure them that sometimes one *single phrase* in the shortest free-write can be the catalyst for the most powerful of plays.

I go around the circle in order of the seats so that there is a random alternation between the more and the less shy readers. I instruct them to read *everything* because the greatest jewel is often the very phrase that the writer feels the least *comfortable* about sharing. (Remember, this exercise is done only *after* spending an hour or so working as a group, and talking about how they will become a Company based on *shared vulnerability and mutual respect.*) After each student finishes reading his or her piece aloud, I praise everyone for their courage and thank them for their trust. I may gently ask them to read certain lines aloud again because much of it will have been read fairly quickly and inaudibly.

If I've written one, and need the practice, I read my own free-write first. If not, I start with one or two of the students who were more comfortable sharing in the Name Game. This allows others to get a sense of what to expect and how to participate. Again, *managing the anticipatory anxiety* is half the battle. As we proceed, I work respectfully and enthusiastically with each student's raw material. I am very careful not to compare their responses. Students generally write short plays, poems, stories, or random free associations. I try to highlight *something of value* in each. I comment on things such as descriptive language, keen observations, a lovely sense of humor, originality, courageousness, and simplicity. I also *thank* each and every student after they finish reading. I am letting them know that I have received their trust as *the gift* that it truly is. For the students who were blocked for a few minutes, the fact that they wrote anything at all is a major accomplishment that should be applauded. For the student who was a wiseguy during the Name Game, the fact that he or she took this second exercise more seriously is nothing short of poetic.

Sometimes a student absolutely refuses to read the free-write aloud. I try to ferret out whether it's for fear of reading, or for fear of sharing what was written. I can assess this by simply asking if *I can read* it aloud. If the student says "Yes," I read it. If the answer is "No," it's usually a content issue. I remind students:

> Everyone has felt vulnerable sharing today. What we write is an extension of who each of us is as a person, and therefore it's inherently personal. Screenwriters bite their nails off at previews of their films—this fear is all too human. But if I collect and read your work privately, I will be the only one who can witness how magically it will transform into a polished play. That is what we are all here to explore.

I conclude by speaking very warmly and personally to someone: "David I can see that this is very hard for you, but I think you can do it anyway. Please try." I have never had anyone fail to respond to this. If I did, I would either collect the piece and give written feedback, or I would meet with him briefly after the class.

Once students have moved on to a Treatment, they might be willing to read free-writes aloud retroactively. At times, there is something deeply revealing in the content, such as intimations of homosexual feelings, memories of childhood molestation, or revelations of sexual exploits. I always ask the writer to change the personal pronoun from "I" to "he or she" and I remind everyone that these are works of imagination.

The Inter-Play that follows the reading of free-writes is a time when students can get a powerful sense of what it is going to be like to dialogue with someone who takes them seriously, who has the courage to ask hard questions, and who can help them find answers. I believe that, now more than ever, they need to sense that I have a great desire to learn about them, and that they are worth all of the time and effort that learning will entail. Figure 2–1 shows a sample Trigger. The next two sections contain a free-write written in response to that Trigger and a sample Inter-Play that followed.

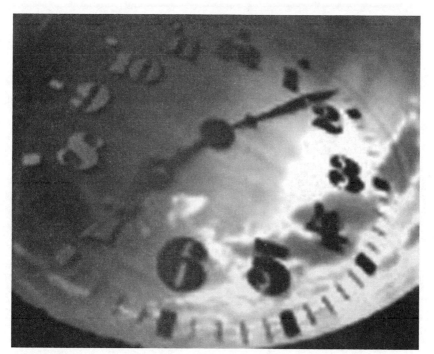

Figure 2–1. Sample Free-Write Trigger ■ *Photograph by Dia Max/Getty Images.*

Sample Free-Write

Time goes by too fast—much too fast. The sun travels overhead at a tremendous speed. The days are too short. We're forced to live as if each day is our last. One day the clock will stop, on a significant moment in our life. We won't know if it will keep ticking, if it will tick forward or backward. Are we in that moment now? Is time standing still? Is it going forward, or backward? There is really no such thing as time, only a series of moments.

—Dan Missale

This free-write was penned in five minutes in response to the Trigger photograph. It is short, but not atypically poetic. A good photograph captures a frozen moment; in its captivity the moment becomes more heightened, which can often evoke poetry in students who don't normally "speak" in that kind of tone. They usually are both surprised and embarrassed by their own language. Then, they hear how many other students responded in that same manner, and how positive the feedback from their peers and teachers is. Once the writer's "gut" response is out there, the task of the teacher is to enter the poetic window the free-write created; he can use it to engage the imagination of the writer in order to find an idea for a play.

The Dramaturgical Inter-Play is one of the most challenging aspects of this methodology, but it is also great fun. It's challenging because there is no real preparation the teacher can do, nor is there an existing map to follow. The only preparation is the student, and his or her free-write is the map. I simply listen with three ears, and then respond as best I can with both my head and my heart. It can be scary, but the antidote to *my fear* is the knowledge that the student's fears are even greater. Another safety net is the knowledge that I can always take the free-write home with me so that I can give further feedback at the next session if necessary. I always try to remember that I am the best role model for trusting and risk-taking in my classroom.

While students are reading their free-writes aloud, I listen for a *key line* that has the potential to open the writing out into a *dialogue between* two people. For me the key line in the preceding free-write was: "Are *we* in that moment now?"; it asks a *question* that inherently begs a *response*. It also uses the plural pronoun *we*, which implies the opportunity for a second character. I share this insight with the student, Dan, and then I begin to approach his entire piece as a potential *scene*. I ask him a series of questions for which he will need to improvise answers since there was no premeditated story idea. This *intellectual improvising* is a real challenge, particularly for nonverbal students. However, students always give over to it *if I participate* whole-heartedly with them, and *if I acknowledge* their initial discomfort.

There's a reason it's called a *play*, but many (young) people have never had the encouragement to play productively. If the photograph serves as the inkblot to stimulate an unconscious response, then the improvisation becomes a kind of *free association* to shape that response. As long as students weave their stories through a character outside of themselves, it will remain play-making, not unintended self-disclosure (see Establishing Trust and Managing Revelation section in Chapter Four). Here is the exchange that followed the reading of Dan's free-write; my comments to you, the reader, are indicated in brackets.

Sample Dramaturgical Inter-Play

Teacher (T): "Clearly the character who is speaking is very anxious about time; running out of it as well as being stuck in it. When they say 'Are *we* in that moment now?' *who* might they be talking to?"

Student (S): "I don't know." [This is always the first response!]

T: "There are no wrong answers here Dan. We're just doodling out
   loud; give it a try."
S: *(After a long silence)* "Maybe it's an older brother."
T: "Okay. *Why* is he feeling anxious?"
S: "I don't know."
T: "Take a guess."
S: *(Silence)* "Maybe he doesn't approve of his brother's lifestyle."
T: "What lifestyle would that be?"
S: "I don't know."
T: "We're just playing. Think out loud; like you did so well in your
   free-write. Tell me about these brothers."
S: *(Pause)* "Maybe the older one thinks the younger one should mind
   his own business, 'cause he's just living his life to the fullest."
T: "*What* might happen if he does, or doesn't, mind his own busi-
   ness? What's at stake?"
S: "I guess the younger one needs him to settle down."
T: "Why?"
S: "I don't know."
T: "You don't have to know; just imagine!"
S: "I don't have an older brother!"
T: "That's okay, this isn't about *you*."
S: *(After a silence)* "The younger one needs him, but the older one
   won't settle down 'cause he thinks this is his last chance. He's
   about to turn thirty."
T: "Terrific."

After this brief exchange, Dan had the underpinnings of a play in
place. He *had identified* two characters and two conflicting *wants*. He
also had some additional thinking to do at home to address:

- The *Passover Question*—why this day might be different from
  all other days for these brothers.
- The stakes—why the younger brother *needs* his brother to
  straighten out.

Dan was then asked to write all of this up as a Treatment—a paragraph
about the story of his play. His Treatment and the play that was subsequently developed are analyzed in Chapter Four, *The Methodology:
Writing and Re-Writing*.

READER EXERCISE

The following is another free-write, also written in response to the
image in Figure 2–1. I invite you to read it, and then to imagine what
comments and questions you might share with the student writer in

an effort to find the seeds of a play. I think you will see that for the teacher as well as students there are *no right answers* here, only *right questions.* The possible responses are infinite. To my mind, what is important is that students have the positive experience of sharing their thoughts. They should also end up with some germ of a play idea with which to begin working. This germ is more likely to emerge if the student is asked to specifically consider: Who is in the story? Who else could enter into the scene? What might each want? How are their wants in conflict? I always make sure that my questions lead back to answers to these questions.

Another Sample Free-Write

> *I don't know what to write. I don't know what to write. It reminds me of a Dali painting with all those melted clocks. Like time being stretched or something. It feels like nobody has time anymore. For anything. It's like there aren't enough hours in a day for people. Everyone seems too wrapped up in cell phones and TVs and computers and themselves. Nothing can go by slowly and when it does people get angry. It's funny you could be walking down the street talking on a stupid cell phone totally oblivious to a beautiful sunset. It's like nature takes the time to paint this beautiful picture for you and people just don't care. They are too busy. Busy, busy, busy. Nobody has time for a sunset anymore.*

> —MaryAnn Hedderson

You may want to write your responses to this before going on to read mine (see page 35). It's ideal if you too can do so in the spirit of a free-write. Jot down whatever comes to mind in any order; see where it leads you, and then collect your thoughts at the end. How did the writer begin? What is the quality of the writing? Is it evocative? Well observed? Is there any potential for character(s) here? Story? Conflict? These are the kinds of notes I take while I listen.

Facilitating Free-Writing. ■ Although your students might be more or less articulate than MaryAnn was in her free-write, there is much that can be generalized to all potential free-writers. What is essential is that the students be respectfully and caringly drawn out a little *before* they are asked to write at Orientation. MaryAnn was originally stuck. When I saw that she was not writing, I approached her. She told me that she didn't "know what to write." I told her that she didn't need to know, she only needed to write: "When you're frozen, don't fight it, accept it. Just describe your feeling, and then describe what your eyes see and what it reminds you of." I encouraged her to trick her brain by starting to write about her block. Then she could write about what she saw in front of her, and then the ink would just keep flowing. It's almost impossible for most of us to relate to things that are completely outside of the context of our own lives, but we can always associate a new thing to a more familiar one. Once we do, we are writing.

You can see that she wrote about her dilemma twice. Then she began to describe what she was looking at. She needed to get past her own resistance to sharing, and her fear that it wouldn't be interesting. This is a student who, despite great natural acting ability, would constantly second-guess herself either by forgetting her lines or her wants. She actually had a lot to say. MaryAnn attended a museum-based high school. She likened the photo to a painting she had recently seen, which clearly had left enough of an impression on her that she even remembered the artist's name. The painting she's referring to is "The Persistence of Memory" by Salvador Dali, which was actually the painter's homage to the unconscious mind!

Once she got going, MaryAnn used the specific Trigger to launch into a more general musing about the quality of life in today's fast-paced world. She describes a world that is often overwhelming, especially to teenagers like herself who are about to take their independent places within it. Many of the props from her life—cell phones, computers, TVs—are mentioned. These are all modes of *virtual communication* that often prevent us from literally connecting. Her intellectual musings finally become a little more personal in the last sentences—*someone* is too busy; *someone* is missing what's really important.

Learning as a Relationship. ■ After she reads, I immediately compliment her on getting past her initial block. And I thank her for trusting my suggestion that she use her pen as a shovel to write her way out of the hole. I then comment that her language is clear and intelligent, and that her images of the painting and the sunset are vivid. I also acknowledge the truth that she was exploring about today's world. After she feels heard and respected, I move farther into the area of her imagination. I speak to her in the tone of one artist to another.

T: "I got a very clear picture of someone busily talking on their cell phone, unaware of a gorgeous red and orange sky. Does someone specific come to mind?"

S: "Not really." [When a student can't immediately answer a question—and this will come up often during the regular re-writing sessions—others in the group may be tempted to answer for them. I don't let them. It is overwhelming for writers of all ages to have other people's story ideas *polluting* their own albeit nascent ones. I gently get the class to understand that this kind of creating-by-committee is not helpful. The stories should *come only from the writer* if they are to be authentic expressions of that person. It is also crucial that the *teacher not impose story ideas* either. It's tempting to do so when a student is blocked and missing some obvious solutions; however, I try to just keep asking questions of the writer as long as I can. If I do help them to articulate an idea that they seem to be implying, I always follow the suggestion with the question: "Does that feel right to you?" If there is any hesitation, I have more digging to do.]

T: "Can you imagine someone who doesn't have time to notice a sunset?" [I want to help her find a potential character as soon as possible.]

S: "Yeah."

T: "How old might they be?"

S: "Maybe around thirty."

T: "Male or female?"

S: "Male."

T: "Would they be successful, a high-functioning person?"

S: "Very."

T: "So their obliviousness is not due to depression, or some chemically altered state of mind?"

S: "No." [Notice that once the issue is unlocked, the answers start to come spontaneously.]

T: "Is he alone, or with someone else?" [I want to find the potential second character as soon as possible as well.]

S: "I'm not sure. "

T: "If someone else were there, would they be disturbed by his obliviousness?" [This will also draw out the potential for conflict.]

S: "Very disturbed."

T: "Might it even threaten their ongoing relationship?"

S: "Yes."

T: "Any idea if the other person is male or female yet?" [I keep returning to the *key* questions until the answers reveal themselves.]

S: "Female."

T: "It sounds like a tense situation; why might her intolerance of his obliviousness be peaking today?" [I also want to get her thinking about the Passover Question.]

S: "I don't' know."

T: "Go back to the image of a clock." [Returning to the *source* is
    always a good focusing device.]

S: "She's thinking that life is too precious to waste."

T: "Why today, more than yesterday?"

S: "I really don't know."

T: "You don't have to know; you only have to imagine."

S: "Maybe someone close to her died recently."

After the Inter-Play, I smile and thank MaryAnn for her willing-
ness and courage to "play" with me. Then, I repeat her Treatment
back to her: "A thirty-year-old man, and the woman he's in a relationship with, are at a turning point. He's too busy and preoccupied
with work and she, having just lost someone close to her, needs time
to just cherish life more." I ask MaryAnn if this is the story she wants
to tell, and she nods. I ask her to go home and write it up. I also ask
her to consider: Where are they? What are they doing? How might this
conflict resolve itself? Although it requires practice to finesse this kind
of exchange, you are halfway there *if your questions* serve the sole
purpose of drawing out two characters and one conflict. MaryAnn
had no set idea for a play before we began, but her free-write contained more than enough to pull from. She was also cooperative during the Inter-Play; that is not always the case.

One student I had, Octavio, never said more than three words at
any session all term. He eventually did fulfill his Monologue and was
ultimately part of a public Presentation, but he wrote exactly two sentences—"I don't like to write. And I don't like that picture."—in
response to a photograph of a fire hydrant with an American flag
painted on it. Among people with communication disorders, this kind
of negative response is not uncommon. When I have very few clues
to go on, because of the writer's resistance, I try to explore the resistance itself. This usually provides insight into what is being protected.
Speaking to him as one artist to another, the intent of my first question was to provoke a constructive response: Any strong feeling is
worth exploring.

T: "Do you dislike the picture because you think it's a bad photo-
    graph, or because you're not patriotic?"

S: "I'm very patriotic."

T: "Did you find the image disrespectful?"

S: "Yes."

T: "Why?"

S: "It's on a hydrant."

T: "And?"

S: "Dogs piss on those."

T: [Everyone laughed at this, and he felt both supported and embarrassed. I quickly invoked the Golden Rule explaining that while
it sounded funny, Octavio was seriously offended.] "Do you feel
that the photographer was being unpatriotic?"

S: "Yes."

T: "I apologize if the photo disturbed you."

S: "I'm used to it." [I always explore vague references.]

T: "To what?"

S: "Everyone dissing the USA." [This dialogue occurred the summer
after 9/11, following the start of the war in Afghanistan. I tried
to veer the exploration away from his personal life.]

T: "Can you imagine this causing a conflict between two people?"

S: "Oh yeah."

T: "Can you imagine two potential characters who are not real
people from your life?"

S: "A guy and his girl, I guess."

T: "How old are they?"

S: "I don't know—eighteen."

T: "Might their differing views threaten to end the relationship?"

S: "Most definitely."

T: "How?"

S: "If he enlists, it's over."

I affectionately point out that he'd had a terrific play in his pocket
and was holding out on me. Then I speak it back to him: "There is an
eighteen-year-old guy and his girlfriend. He is very patriotic. She is
less so, either in general or because of the specifics of a current polit-
ical event. His desire to enlist in the military is threatening to end their
relationship." He nods. I tell him to go home and write it up and to figure out why this conflict has *come up today*. I also ask him to consider
why the girlfriend is threatened by the thought of the guy enlisting. I
remind him that this is not meant to be autobiographical, and that he
should invent names for his two characters.

I have found it to be crucial for the teacher to reiterate the agreed-
upon story idea each time; otherwise, students come back with something that neither of you recognize. I also reiterate the Treatment
assignment several times. In fact, for younger students a worksheet
can be distributed with the following standard questions enumerated:

- Who are the characters?
- What is their relationship?
- Where are they? What are they doing?
- What do they each want?

- How are these wants in conflict?
- Why is this conflict coming up right now?
- How and/or can the conflict be resolved?

When written up in paragraph form, this should yield a very respectable Treatment.

After the first few Inter-Plays, the other class members begin to understand the *rules* of the game. They even begin to prepare answers to the anticipated questions. This is all right with me, as long as they *share* their free-writes as written. I never allow anyone to add more after the pens are put down at the end of the free-write. Once we've all agreed on play ideas, I collect and copy the free-writes. I return them at the following session, and we refer back to them many times over the course of the term. If it's impossible to copy them, I collect and read the free-writes. Then I take some notes and ask the students to bring them to class each time as a reference point during the Workshops.

I also take notes during the Inter-Play. This way I can make sure that the Treatment they bring in, while further developed, has remained true to the original story idea. If there has been a change, such as the gender of the characters, the location, or the resolution of the conflict, there should be a very compelling reason for it. However, the *wants* and the *conflict itself* should stand as they were. It's tempting for students to come up with new ideas for many reasons—perhaps, low self-esteem causes them to second-guess themselves, they're tempted to copy someone else's idea, or maybe they're embarrassed at having communicated too much. None of these, in my mind, are positive impulses; they only prove to further the communication disorder.

If the student does come in with a *new* idea, I don't even begin to assess it. I remind him or her that one of the main purposes of this exercise is to *teach students how* to stick with their initial idea and to learn how to improve it. I invite the student to write up a second idea on his or her own time. I also promise students that they will end up with plays they can be proud of, even if they hated the Trigger. At this point, I might refer them back to the sample play that was included in the Manual—it's a shining example of where they are heading. When everyone in the circle has shared, I compliment them again on their courage and thank them for listening respectfully to one another—now they are on their way to becoming writers. From having collectively survived the ordeal of public sharing, usually there is a "high" in the group. I never rob them of the "victory" by trying to immediately channel their energy into another focused activity. This is the time that I reward them with something that has been selected for them personally—their first Monologue assignments.

FIRST MONOLOGUE ASSIGNMENTS

For my after-school programs, I interview all of the students before the term begins. This allows each of them a little time to learn about me and about what to expect in my class. If the course is voluntary, the interview can encourage the participation of some and discourage the participation of others. I always follow a particular *Interview etiquette.* After establishing a warm and personal connection, I do the following:

- Ask a little about their public and private communication backgrounds: "Have you ever done any acting, writing, dancing, singing, debating?" I assure everyone that these are not prerequisites for the Training.
- Tell them about the re-acting and re-writing Training that I offer. I also describe the outside work that will be involved.
- Ask each of them, based on the previous description: "Does this sound like something you would like to try?"
- If the student says "Yes," I ask the two most critical questions of all: (1) "What do you hope to gain from the Training?" and (2) "What do you feel you could bring to a group?"

For the same reasons as in the Name Game, question (2) will be difficult for most to answer but it's an important first step toward voicing. I have been known to discourage the student who said she could bring her "star quality," while I encourage the student who offers his earnest desire to "stop being afraid to speak up." The Interview also affords me an opportunity to get a sense of students, both physically and emotionally. Based on these observations, I can then select a first Monologue assignment that I think will be comfortable and appropriate. (For recommendations, see the Monologue chart in Appendix I.) In a group of more than twenty students, it's fine to assign the same Monologue to several students. Their interpretations will be as different as their appearances, and their re-acting problems as varied as their personal histories; there's no danger of it becoming too comparative. This repetition also allows the teacher time to learn a few plays very well.

If you have not been able to meet the students beforehand, the distribution of Monologues should be reserved for the second or third meeting during that first week. Toward this end, you can make a brief note or two about each student's appearance and affect, during the first classes, then you can make selections in their absence. You may also want to draw on the information that you gleaned during the Name Game.

The Monologues should all be legibly copied, collated, stapled, and labeled with each student's name in advance. Before I distribute them, I tell students a little about what they will be doing as re-actors by explaining:

- The difference between a Monologue and a Dialogue. (Refer to the Glossary if you forget.)
- That all of thc Monologues were taken from full-length published plays, most of which are available in the library.
- That students will be asked to memorize Monologues by reading them over and over. They will then cover the text with a sheet of paper, trying to anticipate what follows line by line.
- That students will speak the words to a partner from the class, who will represent the other character in the scene.
- That students will eventually feel comfortable behaving as if he or she were the person in the Monologue.
- That this is the kind of exercise practiced by all professional actors in order to learn their craft.

I also tell them that before any of the preceding can happen, students must be able to *comprehend* what the piece is about. They all read their Monologues to themselves, then they ask me to explain any words or ideas they didn't understand. After a quiet reading time, if they raise their hands, I approach them and answer questions privately. Then I get *them* to reiterate all of the meanings we shared.

I've learned that students often say they understand because they're *too embarrassed* to admit that they still don't get it. Also, students with communication disorders don't listen well, so often they don't remember what I've said two minutes aftcr I'vc said it. Before they leave for the day, students should all be able to answer three key questions, which will be asked at the next meeting, about their pieces.

1. *Who am I?*
2. *Whom might I be talking to?* ■ (This is not always clear from a one-page Monologue excerpt, but students should be able to select a logical possibility based on the piece's context. For this first in-class exercise, I think it's more important that their understanding of who the *listener* is be appropriate for the character's want rather than being strictly accurate to the play itself. If a character needs help to achieve a dream, that help could come from a platonic friend, a romantic friend, or a sibling, as

long as there are no textual clues that are contrary to the choice. In later assignments, when students have more time to read the entire play, and to go deeper into character development, the choice should be accurate as well as appropriate.)

3. *What do I want from the person I'm talking to?*

If the Orientation has been spread out over several sessions, I have students read the Monologues aloud at this point rather than waiting for the first acting class. Everyone will probably be nervous about getting up and reading, but by now they have already read their free-writes aloud. I reiterate to the group that they will neither be graded nor judged on this exercise. This is a chance for everyone to hear each other's material, and to practice speaking publicly in a safe situation. I start with a few volunteers, then just go around the circle. I send each student up to the front of the room with a listener, even though everyone's eyes will probably be glued to the page. This provides them with both security and focus. I also direct them to just read intelligently, and to err on the side of slowness; everyone has the tendency to read to someone more quickly than they would speak to them. If they have a small voice, I encourage them to speak so that the listener can hear every word, which allows others to practice their listening skills as well.

While I listen that first time I hold my copy of each Monologue. I highlight or underline anything that the reader clearly didn't understand or mispronounced. Because this takes me away from *reading* the student, I then have them read it a second time with greater clarity. When I address the words and sentences that seemed unclear to each of them, I remind students that these are sophisticated plays and everyone will have some confusion or other. When they've finished reading, I compliment them on their courage, and any other apparent strength, including clear articulation, a strong voice, a nice pace, soulfulness, comprehension of material, focus, posture, and so on. Then, I ask them to describe what's going on in the piece in their own words and to try and answer the preceding three key questions. If they can't answer them, that's okay—this is *not a test*. I share the answers with them by pointing out the clues in the text, then I reassure them that they will get more proficient at doing this each time.

Again, I've found that *reviewing the task* required for the next session is crucial for healthy progress. I instruct each of them to begin learning the piece for the upcoming class, then I remind them of what is at stake for the character in their particular piece: "If you don't help [St.] Joan reverse her sentence, she will be imprisoned for life. It is your job to help Joan fight for her freedom." The more I can *charge them with helping* someone else, the more they can get past themselves.

I close the Orientation by encouraging students to think of themselves now as imaginers, makers, and doers. When they place the Monologues inside of their Manuals, along with their free-writes, they should also begin to think of themselves as professionals. It has been a long day (or days), and one that has presented many challenges.

By the time students leave the Orientation, they should know (1) what they're going to be writing a play about, (2) what their first Monologue assignment is about, and (3) a little about each other. They should also feel seen, heard, and embraced, which are probably new feelings. They might not be sure they like it, so I tell them to be patient and to trust the process. Everything they will be asked to do during the rest of the course will only be a deeper version of what they've already accomplished at this Orientation.

3 The Methodology: Acting and Re-Acting

D uring the session following Orientation, we begin to dig into the actual study of student's first Monologues. Many of you who are reading this book probably have no formal acting training. I would venture a guess that most academic teachers view it as an outlet only for extraverted people. It isn't. In fact the very tenet of *good* acting is the medicine that heals the voiceless. You must take the focus off of yourself, and put it on the person you're talking to. That's why I call it *re-acting*. For teenagers, particularly neglected ones, this is quite a challenge. But if the challenge is met, the result is improved communication. Even if you have *never* studied or taught acting and play-writing, it is my hope that exposure to this perspective will be a helpful tool for you. Remember *re-acting* and *re-writing* are only the *vehicles*; the journey is relevant for teachers and learners of any subject.

Guiding the Voices

I have come to refer to the teachers I train as *Guiding Voices*™; that is what they are, and that is also what they'll be doing. Guiding a voice requires an understanding of the fact that *sharing* spoken and written words is *scary*. Again, to accomplish the goal, you should be prepared to *manage fear*. To do that you must be empathetic, and you must advocate. In other words, you *must help* your students *fight the demons* that rendered them voiceless to begin with. And, you must do it all session long, every session, even if you're tired and beleaguered that day. How is this done? The following are good ways to start.

- *By acknowledging every small step forward.* I have observed that it is difficult for many teachers to lead with *positive feedback* because they are so eager to *fix the problems.* Additionally, they feel like they're lying if they say something too positive. These teachers are watching for the big improvement rather than the small achievements. I've found that resistant learners will not even hear constructive criticism unless they already feel affirmed in some way.
- *By helping them to take risks.* I keep my students in the game gently, softly, lovingly. I don't overwhelm them with enthusiasm either; I am a steady, consistent presence. I'm also a big believer in the healing power of touch; something that has been lost in this all too often child-abusing world. I never hesitate to put a friendly arm around a student who has just survived a big risk.
- *By setting high standards, and being firm about accepting nothing less.* I have seen that lowering a standard is ultimately *more* damaging to a learner's self-esteem than her or his struggling, with my help, to meet a high one.
- *By knowing your subject matter.* If I want students to do their homework, then I must do mine. If I feel stymied during a moment of Coaching, I tell the student that I want to "sleep on it"; then I give them more thorough feedback next time.
- *By knowing your goal, and by making it clear to your students, again and again.* "The goal of this work is to find your voice through re-acting and re-writing—to help you become a better communicator."

In sum, as the teacher of a scary subject, I must *make it safe*. This is done, in part, by emphasizing to the group that acting is a non-competitive team "sport." Everybody will tackle their own demons in their own time. I also stress that work is never bad unless it hasn't been done (in which case I have more fear management to do). If I've been successful, by the end of the course their Presentations will also be of the highest possible artistic merit. The fact that the Training has conquered their communication disorders need not be highlighted. I never speak to my students about them having a problem per se. I simply reassure them that communicating is going to become easier as they get better at it. The crucial thing is to *focus on the craft* itself.

Over the years, I have observed two basic truths about the craft of acting:

1. Good acting is about *truthfulness*, and human beings lie to themselves all of the time.
2. Anyone can be *taught* to act, given the proper tools and the proper encouragement.

When I teach those who have never acted, I actually use the same *conservatory-style techniques* and published materials as I do with adult professionals. I have found that even very young students, and bilingual students, have no trouble understanding the sophisticated plays their pieces might be taken from. After a few big words are defined and pronunciations are reviewed, they primarily struggle with *connecting*—admitting that they want something from someone else. But very slowly over time—after a good *listening environment* has been created: headphones, hats, and attitudes shed—the need to check out is always overcome by the desire to check in.

Once students *are fully engaged* their learning actually happens very rapidly, and it continues even beyond the end of the course. I have worked with many formerly teenage students again several years after they graduated from high school. These graduates always became exponentially more crafted as they matured, even if they never took another class in acting or playwriting after leaving mine.

Studying Human Behavior

So what exactly is it about the study of acting that allows such intense engagement, maturation, and articulation to happen? During their first exposure to acting most students believe that they are going to be *relieved of themselves* and asked to become someone else. Not so. They are actually going to become *more themselves* than they've ever been before, as they learn to interpret someone else's wants through their *own personality*. They will be asked to let themselves be seen being angry, sad, scared, happy, lonely, jealous, vengeful, smitten, bitter, needy, and so on. Frequently, these are feelings that we all try to hide from the world; but students are to have these reactions on behalf of the characters they are portraying. If the character is to express anger, then the student is the conduit for that anger. They are not to express it in exactly the same way anyone else expresses anger, but in the very specific way that they express it.

The characters they will be asked to portray sometimes may seem to be very different from themselves, but to some extent we all have every possible trait within us. Depending on the character, we have to call on a big or a little piece of ourselves. For example, most people have never been Fascist leaders; however, everybody has probably bullied another person at some point, and maybe even enjoyed that power. The impulse simply should be intensified in a situation where the character has a *desperate* need to bully people to get what she or he wants. It is essential that a student never sit in negative judgment of the character being portrayed. The Audience may see Adolph Hitler as a sociopath, but he certainly didn't see himself that way; nor can the student who is portraying him.

In sum, acting is a study of human behavior that implicitly asks students to explore and reveal their own behavior. The Coach makes it safe for them by explaining that they will never be asked, or even allowed, to portray a trait for its own sake. If their character *re-acts* with anger, it's for a reason. For example, if a character is angry because he can't get what he wants, the student then makes a choice as to how to help him get it by: yelling, arguing, threatening, shoving, bribing, and so on. That, *physicalizing choice,* is called acting.

Acting as Doing

I always begin the Training by explaining that the word *acting* means "doing." My emphasis is on *behaving*, not on speaking. If anything, acting requires more *listening* than most people have ever asked themselves to do before. This is because *re-actors are always assessing* the other characters to see whether their behavior is eliciting the desired response. Additionally, to learn to act you must become *act-ive*—be willing to pursue what you want with great *energy*. Even if students know that their characters do get what they want at the end of the play, the characters that they are portraying don't know.

In addition, you must be active as a learner—willing to take ownership of your own craft. I advise students to never do anything I ask them to do *unless* they understand the purpose of the request. If they don't understand the direction, they can't energetically *act* on it; they can only passively comply. This *ownership* is not only essential for their growing acting craft, but it is also essential for their growing self-confidence.

If students are to funnel the wants of another character through themselves, they will be required to get to know their selves better, and to share themselves with others. They will also be required to know others better—to learn the art of *listening for responses* with all five senses. A response can be, for example, a smile, a twitch, a turning away, a leave-taking, and/or a moan. Students must be vigilant at watching and listening to the person that they want something from; then they can re-*act* appropriately. Being this *fully engaged* is the opposite of alienation and is the antidote to anxiety. You can't be detached and focused only on yourself if you're fully focused on and engaged with someone else. However, learning to see and to be seen are two of the most difficult things to do in life. Engagement requires tremendous trust—trust in the teacher and trust in one's fellow learners. This is why I believe that a classroom *must be* a place where people feel safe enough to be vulnerable to each other. Again, to sustain that kind of a learning environment, I always establish and maintain the Golden Rule: No one laughs at anyone's attempt to communicate—ever.

Studying the Play

So how does a teacher begin to apply the basic principles of trust and connection? I must confess that I'm not an advocate of theatre games or trust-building exercises per se. For me, *trust* in the classroom comes through the *teacher's earnest desire to really see and hear* the students. It also comes through their ability to respond to them, and to get them to respond to each other—*authentically.* This is not easy, especially with teenagers. However, *authenticity is* the antidote to communication disorders such as poor attitude, *headphone-itis, jargon-addiction,* and being antisocial.

I teach the craft of re-acting through the study of exciting, well-written, published plays. I then focus on both the story of the play as a whole and the *want* of a character in one particular scene, and that want is always *positive.* For beginning students, I start with an appropriate *Monologue,* rather than a scene, so that I can focus all of my listening skills on only them. For those readers new to theatre terminology, a monologue is a part of a play in which the character speaks for several paragraphs without interruption. (When another character does respond verbally, it becomes a dialogue or scene.) After the Monologue is assigned, I encourage students to read the entire play so that they can understand the character's situation fully. I emphasize that if it takes less than two hours to hear a play performed, than it won't take any longer than that to read one (see the list of suggested material in Appendix I).

If we haven't already done so at Orientation, I spend the first session having the students simply read their Monologues aloud before the group. I ask them to do so with intelligence, but not high drama. I also direct them to try to come away from the page as often as possible so that they can *look* at their listeners. This allows them to start speaking in front of the group without the pressure of memorization, while also getting them used to partnering. When they finish reading, I always ask them what meaning *they gleaned* before I share my knowledge of what the material is about. Even when encountered out of context, students usually have remarkable "gut" insights into a play. These are important first doors into their ownership of the work, as well as a great way to affirm their natural reading-comprehension skills.

UNDERSTANDING THE MATERIAL

Initially we work together to analyze the text. Once they are clear on who their characters are, whom they are talking to, what they want from the other character, and how they will try to get it, students are better positioned to begin memorizing the material. As an example of this, here's a brief analysis of the famous "Romeo, Romeo, wherefore art thou Romeo?" monologue from Shakespeare's *Romeo and Juliet:*

> Juliet is the teenage daughter in the Capulet family. Although she is alone when she speaks the words, everyone is always talking to *someone*. In Juliet's mind she is talking to Romeo. Romeo is a teenage son in the Montague family, a family that has been feuding with hers for a long time. Because they are forbidden to interact, Juliet *wants* Romeo to defy the restriction and become her lover. As she speaks, she imagines romancing and seducing him with her passion, in order to fill him with the courage to rebel.

Although I rarely assign "period" plays to students who are struggling to find their own natural voices, this analysis demonstrates that even Shakespeare's characters are *engaged* in the pursuit of basic positive wants.

COMMITTING THE MATERIAL TO MEMORY

It is almost impossible for anyone to remember something that they don't understand. Even if they manage to, they will certainly not be able to *act* on what they've read. Once they do understand the material, they will be able to commit it to memory with much less difficulty.

When they are at that point, I emphasize over and over again that someone in the group will always be *on-book*—another student holds and follows along in the script—so they can't possibly *fail*. If they do blank out, all they have to do is say "line," and they will receive assistance. When a line *is* called for, a few words are given—read normally, not performed or colored in any way—to get the student back on track. Being the one to stay on-book is a great way for the more verbally reticent members of the group to safely participate. It is also one kind of interaction that can help to build trust between class members.

One reason that early memorization is so crucial is that I ultimately want students to *let go* of the words. The text is simply the vehicle for *creating and recreating* human connections. What is important for making these connections is the *subtext*—the motivation for the words spoken in a play. For example, a character may say "I love you," but really want money not love. He may not love at all but may simply know that saying those words will get him the money. Eventually, the student's focus on *getting* the money will begin to supercede his focus on remembering the lines. I support this shift of focus by reassuring students that the second person who goes up as the listener is going to be responding with authenticity. This listener is, in fact, the *focus* of the scene. That very notion takes the pressure off of a speaker who is reluctant to be the center of everyone's attention.

When they are beginning to learn their material, I always advise students to practice their lines out loud so that the words won't feel foreign once they are off the page. I explain that the more they read and speak the material, the more they will be memorizing it without really even trying to. It is also crucial that they try to analyze the piece's *flow of logic*—the character's strategy for getting what she or he wants. Beyond that, they will simply have to drill themselves by covering the words with a sheet of paper, and then uncovering one line at a time to see if they were able to remember what follows. I assure them that everyone is nervous about letting go of their scripts, and that on their first time up they will only have to *perform as much as they've been able to learn*. I also establish a *running order* before we begin. I allow those who like to *get it over with* to work early on, and those who like to *delay the inevitable* to work later.

After they do work for that first time, I *praise them lavishly* for having had the courage to get up in front of the group at all. Then my feedback always guides students away from a discussion of the *feelings* they might have had. They will feel whatever is authentically evoked in them by the material, as will the Audience. What is crucial is that they remain focused on fighting for what they *want*—as physical a want as possible.

After clarifying the wants again, I give students an *adjustment*—a direction that, when applied, will alter or strengthen either their physical behavior, their want, or their subtext. For example, they may not realize that the character is saying things she doesn't really mean, just to get what she wants. In the process of giving the necessary adjustment to pursue what the characters really want, I also very delicately make students aware that their personal habits could get in a character's way as well. The habits include mumbling, avoiding eye contact, fidgeting, racing, commenting with their faces or giving attitude, and so on. In other words, I help them to better connect.

Coaching Introverts

What follows is an example of how the student's fear, and the teacher's fear-management skills, can interact; it includes some useful Coaching tips.

A shy student, Grace, goes up to the front of the circle to enact a Monologue. The character she portrays is asking her mother's forgiveness for having run away from home. A second student, Liz, listens as the mother. The two are seated in chairs that are diagonally facing each other to enable connection. It is ideal if the student who is speaking sits slightly *upstage*—farther from the Audience—so that he or she can be fully seen by the class and the listener. I also help them establish an appropriate social distance; many people either sit too far away or too close for comfort.

I ask Grace to explain the Monologue's *context*—whom she is talking to, what she wants, and why she wants it. Then I gently invite her to begin. Grace is nervous. She calls for many lines; particularly after the first three that are the most familiar to her. She talks too quickly and focuses on the floor. Her only want at this point is to finish as soon as possible so that she can return to the safety of her seat in the circle.

When she finishes, I *first* praise her for having had the courage to get up in front of us and for having spent time trying to learn the material. I reassure her that each time she goes up, she will remember more. I explain that *everyone*, even professional actors, call for lines when they're first going *off-book*. At this time Grace might attempt to return to her seat. I will try to *ease* her anxiety by acknowledging that it exists, and by demonstrating that I'm not bothered by it. I do this through a humorous statement directed at her demon: "Don't leave, I'm not finished torturing you yet!" She laughs because it is true—it felt like torture to her. She also likes the feeling that I, her soon-to-be-trusted

Coach, might actually be stronger than the demon that has hampered her freedom. I believe that this is how a *trusting relationship* is created.

I then ask her to reiterate what she wants from her mother. I always speak to the students as though they *are* the characters; this helps to keep them from detaching from the activity. She explains, again, that she wants her mother to forgive her for running away. I then ask her how important it is to get this forgiveness because it's crucial for reluctant communicators to understand the *high stakes* involved in dramatic situations. They can then pursue their wants with *energy*.

Grace hesitantly explains that it's important to gain her mother's forgiveness because she wants to come back home. "Yes," I say, "but *why?*" (Why is a question that young people love to ask; with the proper encouragement, they can also learn to love *answering* it! I have found that tapping into natural curiosity is the key to teaching the crafts of re-acting and re-writing—and maybe to *all* teaching.) After a tortured silence she adds, "Because she can't survive on the streets alone." I smile and praise Grace for her keen insight into the play.

I then ask Grace if she feels that Liz—in the role of her mother— forgave her. She shrugs her shoulders and says she doesn't know. I ask her if Liz ever smiled at her, reached out a hand—softened in any way that would indicate forgiveness. Grace shrugs again; she doesn't know. I then gently explain that the reason she doesn't know how Liz responded is because she never once looked at Liz. I tell her that all of the *answers* are on Liz's face. If Liz does not respond at all, then Grace must start *pulling* for the response she wants—that is acting.

I ask her to try again and to really watch Liz this time. I ask her to try to listen for a response. I reiterate that the scene is about her mother and whether she will forgive. I urge her to put Liz in the spotlight, thus taking the heat off of herself. Grace is nervous about trying again. I manage her fear by giving her permission to do only the first three lines—those she knew well. This seems less overwhelming to her, and she agrees to try. Because she tends to race, I also encourage her to speak slowly enough to allow herself the time to scrutinize her mother.

I have found that a direction to simply speed up or slow down is meaningless; the student must understand the *benefit to the character,* not just the Audience. Once students *can control* their own pace, I always explain that the rhythm of a scene is determined by the heart-beat of the character. The more adrenaline a situation induces, the faster the heartbeat. And, when a *slower pace is taken,* it should not be dictated by a mechanical direction to pause. Students need to *take time* when they're waiting for a response, or when they're consider-ing something—*crossing a bridge.* For example, Grace's mother may tell her that she can come home only if she agrees to break off with her boyfriend. Grace will then need a moment or two to consider her decision before she answers.

Interestingly, although I focus on Grace for a good five or ten minutes, the other students in the circle feel very much a part of her learning experience. Because they all share so many of the same issues, it is often easier for a student to *watch how a problem is solved* when it is vividly demonstrated on someone else. And, because the work is so immediate, it is quite riveting to watch. If appropriate, I point out when one student is having a struggle similar to another's. By the end of the term, they all will become very able, and gracious, diagnosticians. Once they can see a problem, and can anticipate the solution, students have begun to achieve mastery of their craft. They also begin to understand that just as they like *their five minutes* of my exclusive attention, so does everyone else.

At this point Grace will have understood all of my directions, but chances are she will not yet be able to *sustain the connection*. She starts out looking at Liz and then her eyes drift back to the floor where she feels hidden from view; I call this the *hit-and-run* syndrome. Each time she does this, I softly urge her to watch and see how Liz is reacting. Although she will get used to working while I'm speaking to her, she will probably forget her lines every time she actually connects with Liz. I have Grace go over the first three lines many times until she can tolerate being engaged. Each time she connects to Liz, I softly acknowledge her genuine successes: "Yes, Grace. That's beautiful Grace. That's it, Grace." When Grace finishes this next effort she immediately looks out to me, her lighthouse in this new ocean of risk. I meet her anxious gaze with my own calm and reassuring one. I telegraph to her that she is on the right course, that I have been watching closely, and that she is safe. As our bond deepens, she begins to feel better and better about communicating.

Eventually this adjustment will have to be sustained over the course of the entire Monologue. In subsequent weeks, I will use several approaches to try to further the connection between Grace and Liz. I might have Grace take Liz's hand; or have Liz try to pull away, and then ask Grace not to allow her to; or have Liz look away, and then instruct Grace to get her to make eye contact again. I employ whatever would be the appropriate action to "marry" to the words and to allow the reluctant communicator to connect. I have found, however, that many noncommunicators have perfected the art of *looking without seeing*. They might appear to be making eye contact but they are oblivious to reactions; I call this the *dead fish-eye syndrome*. The cure is to have the student pull for a particular response on the part of the listener, like getting her to smile. It will probably take many attempts to really engage the student in this way.

At each session when the students get up to work, in addition to having them reiterate their characters' wants, I ask them to articulate what acting problem was identified last time. I ask the same question during the Writing Workshop. This is a crucial aspect in giving students ownership of their learning. If they can't articulate the previous problem, I guarantee that I will see the very same problem again. By the end of the second Showing, the piece should be *more fully memorized.* It should have attained some flow, primarily because the actor will be *in the flow* of pursuing something she wants from the partner. And, that want should have become completely clear.

Now my feedback can begin to focus on *deepening and sustaining* the newly found connection. This requires constant vigilance however, because I have found that most people's communication demons will continue to try, by whatever means they can, to sabotage their own efforts to connect. This can take the form of forgetting lines, letting go of a hand they've been asked to hold, or *throwing away lines*—saying lines' words in a manner that renders them devoid of meaning. That's when I find it important to remember that the critiques while Coaching must always be prefaced by positive feedback and that resistant behavior must be viewed as fearful, not naughty. One high school teacher I trained expressed her newfound understanding of fear management beautifully when she said: "My fondness for teenagers has been renewed. I can hear their pain and then have the heart to assist them. I really think that the secret of teaching *anything* is advocacy."

After several *successful adjustments* over a number of class sessions, the students will now begin to *physicalize* their wants more. Such actions can include grabbing, pulling away, touching, taking a hand, attempting to leave, and so on. They can also begin using relevant props: a suitcase to indicate leaving or staying, a flower as a peace offering, a coat to put on or take off. Whatever they choose should amplify their wants. In a Scene, as opposed to a Monologue, each actor simultaneously pursues his or her own physical wants. They do so either in tandem, or in conflict. For example in Tennessee Williams' *Glass Menagerie,* the son grabs his keys to put forward his desire to leave, while the mother blocks the door to keep him home with her.

Even in a Monologue, however, the listener can be given very clear directions on how to assist in these exercises. They can resist a touch, avoid eye contact, hold on tight, offer a suitcase, discard a flower, and so on. Ironically, if the listener does provide some *ruptures in connection* it will actually help to elicit an even stronger response from the speaker. Although I preach connection, *dramatic tension* is all about conflict and disconnection. This is why it is so crucial for young people to learn to fight for what they want so that they can maintain the kind of connections they need. I encourage them to use their full physical and vocal ranges to try to get what they want. When students have achieved this kind of engagement, there should appear to be a tense invisible rope between the speaker and the listener. Such a "rope" should never hit the ground even, or especially, when silence prevails. It is very tempting for students to *check out* when they're supposed to be listening—to simply wait for their own next turn to speak. People who don't communicate well cannot stay engaged, and *good craft requires* constant engagement. Again, this is why *re-acting* is so helpful to reluctant communicators.

To further enhance engagement, there should be no onstage *unmotivated movement;* everything the students do should forward their characters' wants. For example, since Grace's character wants to be allowed to stay, it would make no sense for her to get up and wander—she should plant herself. One way to assess whether a movement is effective is to imagine watching the scene on a TV with the volume turned off. If you could only see, and not hear the words, would you perceive the basic dynamic?

That is: Would you know who wants something from whom? Would you know how the other person is reacting? Would you know what their relationship might be? When you close your eyes and picture what these actors just did, what moments were the most revealing of the story? It might have been when Grace reached for Liz's hand, and Liz angrily withdrew it; or when Grace knelt and put her head on Liz's lap, and then Liz reluctantly began to stroke her hair. Those would be important physical moments because they illuminate the relationship.

I never put students on their feet until they fully understand what their material is about. When I see a student who is wandering in circles while talking, I am looking at someone who doesn't know how to get what she wants. When I do put students on their feet, I make sure that they really are *planted* with full weight on two feet, ready to act.

Ultimately, I will know whether Grace is working well if I find myself watching Liz. I will try to see if she is going to give Grace the response she so desperately wants. That alchemy can take as many as six Coaching sessions. By then, the words are flowing, the connection is sustained, and the listener has become *the star.* Grace has taken her first truly giant step beyond her communication disorder, and has also begun to learn the craft of *re-acting*. When this transformation has been effected, she will feel a new kind of freedom and confidence—she will have found the power of her own voice.

Coaching Extraverts

This summary about Coaching Grace provided some guidelines for working with a very shy and reluctant kind of participant. Coaches also encounter the flip side of the coin—the student who is *too eager* to perform. As I mentioned in the Introduction, extraverts can also suffer from the inability to truly connect.

When Shahita goes up to work on her Monologue from the *Star Spangled Girl* for the first time, she is filled with nervous energy. She harbors fantasies about becoming a movie star. In her mind, this has little to do with the hard work of becoming a good actor. She is keenly aware of the attention of the class. Unlike Grace, Shahita feels this as positive attention. But like Grace, her hyperawareness of the class distracts her from the true focus of her words—her scene partner. She is just as trapped in a world of her own as Grace was; she wouldn't even notice if her listener simply got up and went back to his seat. She is *acting for her own enjoyment* and has no clue as to what, if anything, she might want, besides attention.

I ask her to share her want. In this Monologue, it is that the Super stop stalking her. Shahita can only describe her *feeling*: "I'm angry." "Yes, but what do you want *to do* about the situation?" I ask. "Tell everyone." By *everyone* she is referring to the Audience; Shahita cannot yet separate the character's needs from her own as a performer. "What will *change* if you tell everyone?" I ask. "I'll *feel* better," she answers. I explain to Shahita that the character she is portraying is scared for her own safety, and she will only feel better if this man is stopped: "You must use your anger to stop him, okay?" She nods, and I invite her to begin.

What ensues is a highly mannered delivery of the words. Every phrase is *scored* with a prerehearsed intonation and a corresponding hand gesture. There is much eye-rolling and sighing, and all in all it is melodrama at its most profound. Not once does Shahita look at the young man who went up to listen as the Super. She is acting on what she *is*, which is angry, rather than on what she *wants*, which is privacy. (This is the same trap that many good actors fall into when portraying a drunk who desperately wants to make it home without falling; they act on the loss of balance rather than the desire to remain upright.) Shahita is animated and energetic—certainly active—though she is no more connected than Grace was. But she and the rest of the class are impressed with her exhibitionism, and this makes it all the more challenging to have to dismantle her misguided notion of what *re-acting* is.

When she finishes, I first praise her for her courage and commitment; her memorization was nearly perfect. I then ask her, again, what she wants. She reverts back to describing a feeling rather than an action that will beg a *re-action*: "To get angry." "That's a means to an end," I explain. "What result are you hoping to effect?" My students often say they want "support" or "understanding," which only begs the further question: Support and understanding for what? What will attaining that support make possible?

After several tries Shahita remembers that she wants "Mr. Cornell to stop." "Good," I say. "Did your listener hear you? Take you seriously? Will he stop?" She stares at me blankly. I point out that in order for her to know the answers to my questions she will have to *watch* him; she will have to *read* him to assess his response. In fact, she will have to wait for his responses *as she is speaking.* She nods, but over several more tries she never looks at her listener for more than a second. She even begins to close her eyes while she talks; a common symptom when those who disconnect are asked to connect. I softly encourage her to let him answer, reminding her that for the character this is a conversation, not a memorized speech. For Shahita however, it is not yet an *inter*-action.

A few tries later she is so rattled that she begins to lose her carefully memorized words and gestures; this is also a typical reaction to having to make the adjustment to connect. While not pleasant, this temporary slippage is essential for growth. Now that the experience has to include someone other than herself, Shahita is completely thrown. I manage her increasing fear by attempting to limit the stimuli. I ask her to focus only on the first few lines, and then I begin to address her *over-acting.* I do this by praising her first: "You have such a rich and wonderful instrument: a strong clear voice, lots of energy, and an expressive face. For you, less is much, much more."

This concept is completely unbelievable to most teenagers, but they eventually like what they see when their peers in the group start working well. I continue to address her in a comforting voice: "You have to trust the power of the text. The Super, and the Audience, will all get the meaning without you *hammering* the important words, or illustrating their meaning with your hands and face. You're working much harder than you have to. Just talk like you normally do, and get him to stop." The preceding underlined words are not intended to be an exact script to be followed for *anyone* who over-acts, though many of them share these characteristics. My response is always dictated by specific observations of each particular student.

Like most over-actors, who are told to do nothing but talk and listen, Shahita becomes visibly and audibly depressed. Her energy is gone because her want—to show off—has been short-circuited. On her next try, she does talk to her listener—where she was all affect before, now she is totally flat. I beg her indulgence and ask her to trust me. I assure her that she could become a very good actress, but she's going to have to learn to share the spotlight. This is a tough moment because the rest of the class also feels that her performance got worse as she was directed to simplify it. It is essential to affirm their reality—they all saw it with their own eyes. I explain that this is only a temporary setback, and that Shahita will emerge with *craft*, which will be authentic; it will be one that she will own, and one that others will admire. I acknowledge that they all have to trust me as I once had to trust my Coaches.

I also find a moment to connect with Shahita privately before she leaves, to put an arm around her physically and spiritually. I reassure her that I understand how difficult it is to give up an old idea of how something is done, "particularly if you've always been praised for being a *drama queen!*" She laughs, but this is a cagey demon to wrestle. Fortunately, all of my students, who are cut off from other people in some way, relish the sensation of total engagement when they finally achieve it.

Over the next few weeks Shahita and I struggled mightily; she was both self-absorbed and a perfectionist. She lost all of her fire before a new one could be lit. It's important for *the Coach not to panic* during this transition. By the end of the term, Shahita began to be both connected and responsive—many sessions after Grace however. This is when it's important to remember that *change is scary*. It happens slowly and in small steps, but those small steps must be acknowledged. Shahita's ability to listen to others soon began to alter offstage as well. She became a fully present member of the Company, and even recognized over-acting in others.

Coaching With Monologues and Scenes

In sum, most students try to communicate either too much or too little, and they both present their challenges. All of the teaching just described took place in the form of a dialogue with the students. I earnestly believe that communication Coaches should try not to lecture; they should primarily respond to what their students do and say. In other words, if they talk less, their students will talk more. Not unlike response-time, which must be allowed for the listener during a Monologue, teachers must allow time and silence during which they can read the response of their class. They should also be prepared to be vulnerable and to confess mistakes. I've often said: "I gave you an adjustment last week that seems to have taken you in the wrong direction; I'd like to try something different today." Also, I try to own up to *my* anxieties: "It's making me nervous that we're approaching Dress Rehearsal and you're still calling for lines. I *don't want* to send a student onstage unprepared. I know that you know the material, so let's see if you can paraphrase your way through it if you get stuck today."

I've found that if I tell them about the feelings that they're inducing in me, whether it's frustration or confusion, the truth will help to free them of their own demons. I might say something like: "Every time you really get in the flow, you stop yourself by giggling. It's tedious to keep going over the same lines. I want you to start *taking yourself as seriously* as I take you, you deserve that." This is another example of *fighting for,* as opposed to fighting with. In other words, teachers must check egos at the door; Coaching is not about demonstrating knowledge or power, it's about creating a relationship with a learner.

In the longer Trainings, once they have made the *basic* adjustments, I have new students work on a second Monologue. They should now be able to focus on a listener and pull for a response. The second assignment allows them to apply all of their newfound skills to material that is not tainted with the blind terror of their first attempts. It is best also if the second piece stretches them in a different direction. For example, if the first piece was a hesitant declaration of their love for someone else, and heavily explored their comfort with vulnerability, the second piece should provide them with ample opportunity to battle. What I choose is also dictated by a growing awareness of their *issues*—the things that they *shy away from.* For some this may involve showing anger; being humorous, for fear of being laughed at; being physical, sincere, or sensual; appearing intellectual; and so on. I select a piece that will give a "weak note" on their personal keyboards the opportunity to grow stronger.

Students will have *fulfilled* the second piece when they've memorized it, achieved flow, comprehended and achieved the character's want, physicalized choices, and made the partner the star. If time allows, they are now ready to tackle a *Scene* (see sample schedule options in Appendix II). Again, the choice of both the scene and a scene partner reflects my growing knowledge of what they can handle. It also reflects what they need to learn to handle. This gets trickier when *two sets of* student *needs* must be accommodated; but there really are a fairly limited number of *major issues* that come up with almost every weak communicator. These issues include avoidance of connecting to others, discomfort with one's own physicality, speech problems, and/or inconsistent concentration and commitment. Pairings are fairly easy to make. For example, if a male and a female student are both physically awkward and self-conscious about connecting, then a love scene (as in *Hatful of Rain*) is just the challenge they need. If two boys, one tougher and one more sensitive, are both struggling with fighting for things, then the battle between the brothers (also in *Hatful of Rain*) would serve well (see "Casting Suggestions" on the list of Suggested Monologue and Scene Assignments in Appendix I).

Most students find scenes easier to memorize than Monologues because they only have to retain one or two lines at a time, and these lines are directly responsive to what the partner has just said—if they're listening. However, because the person that he or she is speaking to is no longer just a listener, the fear of intimacy may become all the more magnified. Fortunately, by this time students will have developed some craft—their focus on what the other person is saying and doing will begin to override personal discomforts. Ultimately, the scene partner becomes a buddy in the "sea of risk-taking and exposure" that *re-acting* requires.

Halfway through the longer Trainings I schedule a public Presentation of the in-class exercises. By this time, everyone should be so focused on scene partners—and the responses they want from them—that the presence of an Audience will be almost irrelevant. I usually invite a *small group* of other students to watch them present their strongest scenes or Monologues. This is a gentle way of beginning to go public while still in the safety of the classroom. One sign that they are now fully engaged is that they never are tempted to break the *fourth wall*—a theatrical term that refers to the open space between the stage and the Audience. In a classroom, it is the space between the two students who are working on their scene and the rest of the class. When they get past their anxiety about the negative judgment of onlookers, students also *have mastered* their first giant step into successful public speaking.

Crossing the Bridge

Acting is a complex art form, and one that takes years to master. This chapter is meant to serve as a guide to understanding the *basic* craft for use in helping poor communicators. More nuanced work can then be built on this foundation. It is my belief that *connecting* is the very bedrock of good acting, and it must be applied to every Monologue, scene, or play that is studied. And when this way of working is consistently applied, students will inevitably become more present, less lethargic, more articulate, more sociable, and more communicative—in sum, *more literate.*

If you haven't acted before, and didn't take my Workshop before attempting to teach this methodology, *you* should probably try to learn a monologue. *Star Spangled Girl* is a good choice for beginning females, and *Children of a Lesser God* is good for beginning males (see Suggested Monologues in Appendix I). You should memorize it so that you can perform the monologue off-book for a friend. Ask that person to stay on-book for you. Then see if she or he can guess whom you are talking to, as well as what you want. If possible, a second friend should sit as the listener so that you can practice connecting. This listener should be instructed to let you know whether he or she ever feels you're talking *at them* rather than *to them,* or whether they have any idea of what you want. At the end of your monologue, ask the listener what he or she wanted to do or to say as a result of what you did and said; that response should match your want.

For instance, in the monologue in *Star Spangled Girl* you want to be left alone. If you got your listener to take you seriously, which will require working against all the humor in the style of the material, she might want to either apologize, say "okay," or get up and leave. In the *Children of a Lesser God* monologue, you want your wife to speak. If you've made sure that the listener playing your deaf wife was able to read your lips at all times, she might say "okay." In fact if she says anything, you've impressed on her that you want to know her better by hearing her voice. This unsupervised experiment will not teach you to be a *re-actor,* but it will certainly teach you how difficult the study of this craft is!

Once you understand the basic concept of fear management, you are equipped to Coach a student past the fear of public sharing. Again, this is done by connecting someone to another person and then embracing the effort. When you understand that *working well* means focusing your students on the person they want something from, and then going after it, you can use the Suggested Monologues and Scene Assignments list in Appendix I to select the ones to use. This list was culled from the materials I have found to be most effective during my twenty years of teaching young people. It also provides a wide cross-section of styles and stories for students of both genders and all backgrounds. Because it would have required a book unto itself just to print all of these pieces, I have simply indicated where they can be located. I have also shared my knowledge of what kind of student can benefit the most from each piece, and the want that they should be pursuing. It is only meant to be a starting point. For a true understanding of the material, you will eventually need to read all the plays you assign material from.

4 The Methodology: Writing and Re-Writing

T his chapter outlines the methodology for helping students to write their plays, which happens concurrently with their study of published plays in the *re-acting* classes. I provide examples of the following:

- A Treatment—based on one of the triggered free-writes and Inter-Plays presented in Chapter Two—as well as the questions that were asked to help draw a strong play out of the Treatment.
- An early draft of the play, with examples of feedback.
- The play's draft that went into *Table-Work.*
- The final draft of the play, which was subsequently rehearsed and performed at a public Presentation.

Establishing Trust and Managing Revelation

One of the reasons that I have found an *integrated approach* to the study of re-acting and re-writing to be so successful is that these crafts require many of the same basic principles. Like the re-*acting* Coach, a re-*writing* Coach (or Dramaturg) tries to help students articulate *who* the characters are, *what* they want, *why* they want it and what obstacles might prevent them from getting it, and *how* obstacles can be overcome. Once students are able to answer these questions about their story, they will already have the healthy underpinnings for a play in place.

However, as with the study of re-acting, this is all far easier to imagine than to do. Writing, and what you choose to write about, are both very revealing of oneself. If you have never been encouraged to reveal strong ideas and opinions, this is scary indeed. Even if a play is ostensibly telling a fictional story about invented characters, our inventions—much like our acting interpretations—are extensions of ourselves. They reflect hopes, fears, fantasies, and even prejudices. A psychologist once explained to me that it didn't matter whether his patients really dreamt the dreams they reported to him; what mattered was that the content—whether considered while asleep or awake—was important to those patients. *Imaginings reveal* a window into one's soul.

For the purpose of finding voices, it is crucial that whatever *is revealed* by the student be responded to strictly in terms of its potential for good play-making, never as autobiography. As in re-acting, this emphasis takes the focus off the one who is afraid of being seen. For example, a teacher might be tempted to explore a student's personal motivation for writing about a suicidal teenager. I strongly believe that the student should be not asked if he is feeling suicidal, that would only drive him back underground; or it could open up a discussion that the teacher is not equipped to handle. I've had great success when I simply try to ascertain *why* a play's character is suicidal, *what* the character hopes to accomplish by committing suicide, *who* the character wants to affect by that choice, and what *other* choices the character might have.

The healing effect of dramaturgy is that while the depressed student considers some more positive wants in the character's life, he also begins to discover some in his own. Plus, in the process, students will have learned how to craft a piece of healthy writing. It is equally important that students who try to cling to the *exact details* of their own life events remember that their purpose is only to craft literate pieces of writing. Allowing anything more would be irresponsible on the part of the teacher, and would have the reverse of the desired effect.

We are trying to *make it safe* for students *to speak in their own voices,* without rendering themselves intolerably vulnerable in the process. Although *public speaking* is the number one fear in the world, committing something of one's own expression to paper, and knowing that it will ultimately be *shared publicly*, is simply a less immediate version of the same terror. This is why all writing students find their own on-paper version of "staring at the floor"—when they want to hide. This hiding can present itself as anything from the total inability to write anything at all; to the direct imitation of another student's style or story; to the use of a false voice that sounds melodramatic; to overuse of jargon; to a kind of perfectionism that forces them to keep starting over so that the writing never has the chance to improve; to a persistent absence of grammar, which makes what they've written impossible to follow. Interestingly, when students *are ready* to communicate, they are capable of learning the proper use of grammar very quickly.

Applying the Find Your Voice™ Approach

As with re-acting, teachers need to make it *safe* for students to communicate effectively and authentically and, at the same time, give them the tools to do so. The following are some basics of the approach to writing that is being demonstrated throughout this book; it was designed to override the inner demons that prevent students from writing.

- *Use a photo as a starting point.* The photo should be gender, age, and ethnicity neutral; in other words, it should capture an object or a place that can *speak to anyone* (see Chapter Two).
- *Instruct students to write freely in response to the photo.* This will also help provide insight into what they really want to write about.
- *Have students develop a Treatment, which should grow out of their free-write.* This is to serve as a template for the play they will be writing and *re-writing* until their first vision is fully realized. It will also keep them from starting over and over again.
- *Have other students in the group read the drafts aloud.* This enables writers *to hear* whether the writing sounds unnatural, ungrammatical, or derivative of someone else's style. In other words, it keeps the writing authentic.
- *Use an ongoing Workshop approach.* This enables the students to hear each other's styles, and it reinforces the assertion that everyone tells their own story in their own way. Sharing in a Workshop also illustrates the fact that everyone struggles with their own difficulties in doing so. The goal is to keep writing a noncompetitive "team sport."
- *Use Table-Work prior to rehearsing for a public Presentation.* This allows student actors and the teacher to sit and discuss questions about the play. It eventually leads them to authentic and credible dramas—ones that reflect their own fully fleshed-out beliefs about people and situations.

No matter how well charted this journey might be, the writing of an original play still requires great courage and great discipline. Plays aren't written, they're *re-written*. It is very difficult for students to accept that this is something they cannot possibly *get right on the first try*. This is particularly true of those with communication disorders; usually, they are perfectionistic to the point of paralysis. Ironically, the reality that they will have second chances to address unresolved problems in subsequent drafts ultimately becomes the most liberating of concepts.

During twenty years of leading reluctant communicators to successfully express themselves on paper, I've developed some guidelines. The following are the ones I have found to be the most useful for those who are *new* to writing plays, and include the reasons why I endorse them.

Writing Guidelines

Students should do their free-writes quickly. This tends to overpower their inner censors. Erasing and editing can be reserved for subsequent re-writes; the first draft is research for the finished play.

Plays should be short. Having no more than five to ten pages eradicates the tendency for repetition. (A trick that school composition writing unwittingly perpetuates is the discovery of multiple ways to keep repeating the same thing in order to meet the required number of pages set for an assignment.) A satisfying *short* play is actually much more difficult to write than a satisfying *long* play because there is very little time in which to say something of depth. Every word must be essential to the story. I have never seen a more effective focusing device, especially for those learners who mistrust their own expression ability, than to have to be brief and crystal clear.

Speeches within the plays should be short. While long monologues can be riveting in the hands of a sophisticated writer, they are difficult for new writers to wield because they often lose the *purpose* of what they're saying. As an exercise in retaining focus, it is incredibly helpful for students to be sure that every line of dialogue they write is directly responsive to the line that came before it. One of the most common problems in students' writing, and speaking, is that they move from one idea to another with no *cause-and-effect relationship*. Ironically, *their inability* to sustain concentration is then *transferred to us,* the Audience.

Students should explore something they feel passionately about. A spontaneous response to the Trigger is usually good evidence of this. However, as they weave this initial impulse into a fully drawn story, there is often the tendency to either intellectualize or exaggerate the original idea. Students do this for two reasons: (1) as a way of protecting themselves from any revelation of their true feelings; and (2) because they fear that simplicity is boring, they try to embellish. Both responses are only extensions of the fear that *being seen* will lead to rejection and humiliation.

Plays must have conflict in them. Conflict is the single most essential ingredient of drama, even if it is an *inner* conflict. Ironically, as much as young people like to rebel and resist, they all seem to find it difficult to establish and sustain conflict. It is particularly crucial for them to be able to do this when it involves *fighting for* because that leads to a desired *positive* outcome. One of the most frequent problems I have encountered in new writing is that the conflict, if clearly established at all, dissipates almost as soon as it begins. The characters are either overly compliant, or they run away from the battle before any change can be effected. One antidote to this loss of dramatic tension is the *rule of three*—never give characters what they want until they've asked for something at least three different times.

There must be urgency in the play. Said differently, it must be clear that the event in the play *had to happen,* and that it had to *happen now.* I like to refer to this dynamic as the Passover Question—or, why is this day different from all other days? For example, in *The Wizard of Oz,* Dorothy's emotional journey had to happen that particular day. Mrs. Gulch's warrant to remove Toto forced Dorothy to run away from home before anyone could discover that the dog had come back. Her act of running away then led to her being knocked unconscious by the tornado, and to dreaming about her fears of leaving home.

Encourage students to stay with contemporary people and activities. I do this for the same reason that I refrain from assigning material from period plays. The focus of this training is to *help students find their authentic voices;* this is difficult enough to do without introducing language and circumstances about which they can have only a remote and intellectualized understanding.

Limit the number of characters to no more than the two who are central to the story. It is quite a challenge to establish fleshed-out people in a short play. The more characters there are, the weaker all of their portraits will become. In addition, it often serves to lessen the tension between two people in conflict when a third or fourth party is *polluting* the battle with their input.

Limit settings and time frames as much as possible, preferably just one. Today's students are almost exclusively influenced by films and TV; they cannot conceive of a form that doesn't allow for cinematic camera pans, close-ups, and *jump-cuts.* In theatre, the Audience sees everything that the actors are doing in *real-time* and in one space. This reality usually has to be reiterated many times during the early drafts. Again, we are striving to *help* new communicators to *achieve focus and flow.* In a short play, students shouldn't waste time on scenery shifts, multiple lighting cues, or costume changes. All of these pursuits, like unmotivated actor movement, will only prove to muddy characters' connections to one another.

Exposition should also be kept to an absolute minimum. The Audience should learn about characters through the manner in which other characters view them, or from their behavior, not from background information that is simply told. For example, Charlie shouldn't have to tell us he's in love with Suzanne. We should be able to draw that conclusion from the fact that he brought her flowers and waited an hour for her, from the way that he looks at her and touches her. Like pictures, actions can speak a thousand words. One of the mantras I use is *"Show, don't tell":* If the stage directions indicate that Charlie slams the door and then barks a response to his wife, we'll know that he's grumpy. We also don't want characters to tell each other things that they should already know: "Your birthday, *March 18,* is coming up soon." I have found that when student writers can get their characters to be clean and clear, they will also become that way in the process.

Plays should be specific. Another favorite mantra of mine is: *"God is in the details."* We don't go to see a play about a generic traveling salesperson; we go to see a play about Willy Lohman. The more students dig into their specific observations of the world, the more of their own voice will be unearthed. If the story is told well, it will rise from specific to universal without the author consciously attempting to do so. People will connect to the story because they will recognize something of their own experience within it, even if it's a fantasy. For example, *Peter Pan* is about a very specific boy who flies to a very specific imaginary island, but everyone has wished to stay a child forever.

The *emphasis* of this methodology is on *re-writing*. It is extremely helpful for students to have access to a computer at home, in school, or at a library to make editing easier. If computer access is not possible, students should be told to print neatly. They should also be given a sample manuscript format to follow. (The play later in this chapter should serve that purpose.) This format enables those who are reading the scripts aloud for them to easily find their own lines. It will also help them distinguish between words that are to be spoken *(lines)* and those that are to be physicalized *(stage directions)*. The cleaner the format, the smoother the reading will be. Students can then get a good idea of what is, and what is not, working in their plays.

Establishing the Workshop

I suggested earlier that plays should be developed using a Workshop approach. This implies that a group of *supportive* listeners and respondents will be witnessing the birth of each play. When it is guided well, a Workshop is a wonderful way for a student to receive immediate feedback. It is also an opportunity to encourage reluctant class participants to practice their communication skills. They do this by developing more confidence in their own ideas under the guise of being helpful to someone else. Not unlike putting the focus on the listener when performing a Monologue, the timid respondent can be *totally focused on giving assistance* to the writer. Students should be encouraged to make sure that their comments are understood, and that they are helpful. I also enforce the following rules to ensure just that.

Workshop Rules

Feedback should always refer to the play, *never* to the student writer.

Likes and dislikes are *irrelevant.* Respondents should limit themselves to questions that the student can address in a subsequent re-write—such as "The battle was just getting exciting, why did the aunt have to leave so quickly?" Such a question lets the writer know that the aunt/nephew scene is a strong one. It also presents a problem; the scene is too short, and this problem has a *manageable solution:* The student can write more dialogue for them so that the battle is extended.

Explain *how* to use additional stage time. At this point, the teacher can suggest ways to fill other existing holes in the play. This way the writer won't add a page, what I like to call *hamburger helper,* simply to make it longer. If the nephew's attempt to strangle his aunt later in the play seems unjustified, we could learn something in the extended scene that will help us to see the depth of his rage.

Encourage students *not to respond* to feedback by arguing, disproving, or becoming defensive. They should simply take notes. There is usually a little validity in even the wackiest of questions. It's also good practice for poor communicators, who live in terror of negative judgment, to listen to feedback. However, the teacher must provide a safety net by helping the new writer determine what is probably widely felt, and what can be disregarded as idiosyncratic. If a student does start to argue, I lovingly put a hand out and stop her or him. I reassure students that I know how difficult it is to just listen, and that I am there to *protect* both their work and their feelings—from the Treatment through to the final Polish.

What follows is a sample Treatment that Dan developed after the Inter-Play that was summarized in Chapter Two.

Dan's Sample Treatment

THE PERFECT DAY

This is a play about two brothers: Alan (seventeen) and Andrew (twenty-nine). They spend a lot of time together. Andrew thinks this is his last chance to really live. Alan wants Andrew to stop drugging and drinking and to settle down; he's afraid of being sucked into Andrew's lifestyle.

The writer had clearly gained insight into what the older brother's objectionable lifestyle was, but we still don't know *why* Alan needed Andrew to change so much. Why was Alan afraid that he might get sucked in? There was enough of a structure here to begin with though, so Dan was encouraged to discover the rest as he began to write the dialogue. I would have to remain vigilant in ensuring that he *did discover* this as-yet-unidentified need. Still to be discovered too was the *significant moment* referred to in the free-write, but the chosen play title suggested that Dan was planning to frame his story through that lens.

I also had an additional concern that the characters' names were too similar; as the group listened, we all kept getting confused about which brother was which. This is often a sign of a lack of *character dif-ferentiation* in the writer's mind. Because we were not yet clear on what Alan wanted, Dan was urged to make sure that he really had *two* clear characters in mind. As it turned out, the lack of differentiation continued to be a problem. It was ultimately resolved during Table-Work when the students who were cast in the play had to flesh out their characters' biographies. This chain of events is tracked throughout the rest of this chapter.

The first draft of Dan's play was only a single page—as with student actors, most either under- or overcommunicate—but it demonstrated some key things. Dan was indeed allowing the two characters to begin talking, but they were not well enough differentiated. I suspected that he really wanted to be writing about a father but was disguising him as an older brother. (Note the last line of the first draft that follows.) I remembered that during the Inter-Play Dan said he didn't "have an older brother"; he was clearly struggling to invent a story as compelling as the one he didn't want to tell.

The next section leads you through the often challenging process of managing a writer's fear to effect change in the play. It is a process that induces frustration in the teacher and the student. As you read closely through these multiple drafts—and bear in mind they were done over many months—you will have to exercise the very persistence and discipline that was required of the student. I think you'll find that Dan's play gets easier and more enjoyable to read as he improves it. (To practice your own dramaturgical skills, you can download a companion Teacher Workbook from **www.heinemann.com/findyourvoice**.)

The First Draft of Dan's Play

THE PERFECT DRUG

ANDRE
What are you doing.

ANDREW
I'm having another one.

ANDRE
Why. Aren't we going to the pub later.

ANDREW
Okay, Dad.

ANDRE

Shut up. <u>I'm just concerned.</u> You got
pretty plastered last night—

ANDREW

<u>Why are you being so antagonistic?</u> I
think I can control myself.

ANDRE

Can you? Last night you <u>told me you</u>
could barely walk up the stairs
<u>because you drank so much.</u>

ANDREW

There is nothing wrong with being too
drunk to <u>fuck</u> every now and then. You
do the same thing sometimes <u>anyway</u>;
I don't get on your back about it.

ANDRE

I'm still a kid <u>though</u>; I'm allowed to
behave that way.

First Draft Feedback to Dan

Dan, I see that you changed the title; it was *The Perfect "Day"*
in your Treatment. For next time, please answer the
Passover Question. And, although you did change the
younger brother's name it's now even more similar than
before—there's only a one-letter difference!

You also need a stage direction at the top to indicate
that Andrew is snorting coke prior to Andre's first line; then
we'll understand what Andre is reacting to. (It really helps if
you try to visualize character behavior, even if the students
who eventually portray these roles don't follow your exact
stage directions.)

You need to address the lack of punctuation as well. Your
two readers didn't know which lines were questions, or what
was meant to be sarcastic. You'll notice that I've underlined
certain language; it is implied without you having to state it.

Lastly, regarding the profanity, although I encouraged
you not to edit yourself on your first draft, it will become distracting in later drafts.

All that said, this draft is only about a page long, yet the want is beginning to emerge. Andre wants a parent (see your last line). He wants his brother to be more mature so that he's free to be a kid. He wants someone to set limits, and to be a role model. Good job Dan! Now let them keep talking to each other until the battle comes to a full boil; then we can see how it resolves itself.

Dan's play is really very subtle, as many teenagers' plays are. It's not merely a story about one straight-laced brother trying to change a wild one; nor is it a story of a dropout brother trying to get in the way of a college-bound one. As it turns out, the play is not going to be about the older brother's last chance to be a kid, but the younger brother's last chance.

For me, analyzing a play is like analyzing a person: You have to be one part detective, one part psychologist, and one part labor coach. The detective looks at the textual *evidence* (what is there), as well as the *clues* (what's not there) to find the story. The psychologist *listens* for the why, who, and how, *to discover* what story the writer really wants to tell. The labor coach *encourages* the writer until the "child" is born. It takes practice to be able to do it all well but, more important, it takes a burning *desire to really see and hear* your students. I have found that there is nothing more empowering to learners than the time and attention of someone who believes that they have a story worth understanding, *and* one worth telling. The quality of your attention, more than anything, will demonstrate the *craft of listening.*

Dan received this kind of specific feedback and encouragement for many weeks; a later draft follows. Because it was a *later draft,* my comments that follow it raised several problems for him to address.

Fourth Draft of Dan's Play

THE PERFECT DRUG

(ANDRE and ANDREW are sitting in ANDREW's living room. They are getting ready to go out to their neighborhood pub. ANDREW opens up a bag of coke, makes a line and snorts it.)

ANDRE
What are you doing?

ANDREW
Fueling up.

                    ANDRE
Why. We're fuckin' goin to the pub
now.

                    ANDREW
I want one for the road.

                    ANDRE
Take it easy with that stuff tonight, I
don't want to have to carry you home
like last time.

                    ANDREW

(Sarcastically)

    Yeah, all right "Dad."

                    ANDRE
What the fuck do you mean?

                    ANDREW
Calm down bro. Why the fuck are you
being like this?

                    ANDRE
You have been hitting pretty fuckin'
hard on that stuff lately. <u>I just think</u>
you should take it easy.

                    ANDREW
Dude, it's not your concern—

                    ANDRE
Yes it is—

                    ANDREW
No it isn't dude! <u>Worry about your own</u>
<u>fuckin' life for a change</u>, and stop
worrying about <u>others</u>. I know you
think you're helping me out or
whatever, but you're just avoiding
your own fuckin' issues.

ANDRE
I'm your brother. Your issues are my
issues.

ANDREW
Bear with me for a second because I'm
going to give you some tough love.

ANDRE
Go ahead.

ANDREW
You need to be a little bit more selfish.
<u>Worry about yourself more.</u>

ANDRE
Stop avoiding the criticism.

ANDREW
What?

ANDRE
You think I'm only looking after you
and being an exasperating parent like
figure even though I'm twelve years
younger than you? As much as I would
like to say that I am doing this just for
you, I'm not. You have been my father
when dad wasn't there and . . . you
know . . . I'm thankful for that . . . but
because of that . . . I see a lot of you in
myself. And I don't want to be like you
or dad, I don't want to turn to some
sort of drug when things aren't going
well.

ANDREW

(Sarcastically)

That's what you think I do?

ANDRE
Yeah.

ANDREW
You clearly don't know what you are
talking about bro.

ANDRE

(Snaps)

Yes I do.

ANDREW
No you don't <u>dude</u>. It's your fuckin'
choice what to make of yourself. <u>Don't
worry about what other people's effect
on you will be.</u> The sooner you
understand that, the sooner you'll be
at ease.

(Brief moment of silence)

ANDRE
I need you to be there for me. I need
to have you in my life. I need a brother
to look up to.

ANDREW
I'm always here for you bro... you can
look up to me. I'm not going
anywhere. I don't know why you have
this fear of me leaving you.

ANDRE
I'm not scared that you are going to
leave me. I'm more scared that you
will stick around.

ANDREW
What do you mean?

ANDRE
I know I can always look up to you,
but look what I'm looking up to. A
coke addict and an alcoholic. And I
see myself becoming the same thing.

ANDREW
What do you mean?

ANDRE
I notice myself drinking a lot for no
reason at all.

ANDREW
That's your fault!

ANDRE
<u>But</u> you don't see that you are the cause
of me falling into the trap. You don't
think you're an influence in my life.

ANDREW
I'm absolutely an influence. But I
choose what to teach you. I never said
"Hey this stuff is great try it."

ANDRE
That's bullshit.

ANDREW
What?

ANDRE
I said that's bullshit! I see you do
things and then I want to do them too.
You don't have to say anything.

(HE picks up the bag of coke.)

This shit is fuckin' killing us!

ANDREW
Put that down!

ANDRE

(ANDRE pours it on the table and begins to snort it.)

You see what you're doing bro?

(HE snorts some more.)

This is what you're doing to me!

ANDREW

Stop it!

(ANDREW gets up and lifts ANDRE's head up.)

I said stop it!

ANDRE

I need you as a brother.

ANDREW

I'm always going to be your brother.

(THEY look at each other for a long period of silence. ANDREW hands ANDRE a beer.)

Here bro have a beer...alcohol...the
best fighter against drugs.

(ANDRE takes the beer. ANDRE hugs ANDREW. ANDREW gives no hug in return.)

LIGHTS OUT

Fourth Draft Feedback to Dan

Dan, the conflict is much stronger now, and you are starting to visualize their physical behavior very well. We still have some things to clear up. The similar names remain unchanged, and we now have a stage direction, which indicates that they're in "Andrew's living room." The fact that you've mistakenly indicated that they don't share this home again makes me wonder if Andrew is a brother or a dad—note the large age difference referred to on your third page. You're going to have to make a choice. There is also still a lot of profanity; can you develop the reasons for their anger? I noticed a new slang tone coming in; I've never heard you speak this way. Is this really your authentic voice? While you're listening for that, you should also (1) start trying to contract words as you would while speaking, and (2) start eliminating lines that are repetitive—I've underlined several. Finally, there are still some logic problems:

- *Does* Andrew turn to drugs when things get bad? If Andre really doesn't know what he's talking about, Andrew should either set him straight or dodge the attack more clearly.
- Is "I need you to be there" really responsive to the line before it?

- When Andrew grabs the cocaine away, is he trying to protect his coke or his brother? He is never protective of him anywhere else in the piece, and it doesn't mesh with his behavior at the end.
- You still haven't addressed *why* Andre needs his brother to parent him so much. Where are their parents?
- The ending reflects all of these confusions. Why would Andre initiate a hug—he didn't get what he wanted. And why would Andrew not hug back—he *did* get what he wanted.

Dan, the play has come such a long way. There's a lot of potential here, but we'll need to resolve these questions by the end of Table-Work.

Continuing the Dialogue

I decided to present Dan's play because, despite his resistance, he had created a strong piece. Only two major elements were lacking (see The Elements of a Completed Play section in Chapter Five): He needed to further clarify the characters' wants, and he needed to answer the Passover Question. I trusted that we would be able to do this together. Once the play was cast, the two boys playing the brothers read it aloud for Dan and me; I was now the *director* (see more about the role of a director in Chapter Five). When they finished reading, and after Dan was praised for the strength of his work, we began to dialogue about the play. I asked very particular questions of the readers so that Dan could see how well his story had been conveyed. Student writers are always welcome to amplify and clarify information as needed, but this is an important opportunity for them to hear feedback on what is already in the play, and what is not yet in the play.

QUESTIONS FOR TABLE-WORK: FROM GETTING
STARTED TO FINALIZING

No matter how long the Table-Work session is to be, I always begin with a question addressed to the two student actors: "What is this play *about?*" After each answers from their own character's perspective, we move on to the specifics of the story. We check to see if their take on the play is supported by the text. This can also become a *Worksheet*; participants can start on it prior to a Table-Work session:

- Whom and what is this play about? (How do you know?)
- What do the characters want? (Why do they want it?)
- Why does this present a conflict? (Where is that seen in the play?)
- How is the conflict resolved? (Why?)
- Why is this conflict erupting today?

If any answers aren't clear, we ask the student writer to enlighten us. If they are stymied, they either have some quick thinking to do with my help (in a shorter Training), or they have some homework to do. In a yearlong program, Table-Work can take up to three half-hour-long sessions per play. In an academic setting, sessions can be held while other participants prepare their own Worksheets, or they can be scheduled after school as part of the demands of preparing for the Presentation. The goal is to *work out all of the glitches* that reveal themselves when fresh eyes come to read a new play. This perspective is so important because even the most experienced teacher will grow myopic after reviewing five drafts of the same play. This is especially true when it was initially a milestone to get that writer to write anything at all.

What is essential is that the "baby not be thrown out with the bath water." Having come this far, the last thing we want is for students to lose their plays in the home stretch. This can happen if they introduce whole new plotlines, change the personality of a character, or introduce a major new event with inadequate time to develop its ramifications on the rest of the existing script. The trick is to help the student *keep the best and lose the rest;* this can only be accomplished by *restraining* them *from overcorrecting.* For this reason during extended programs, I always have the previous session's draft at hand. This way I can see if anything good has been omitted during the latest re-write. A new script, with all of the changes incorporated, is then circulated at the next Table-Work session.

In the intense three-week, but still thirty-hour program, where the play certainly will only be read and not memorized, the hour of Table-Work is where all of this re-writing will happen. What follows are the five questions that I used for Table-Work on *The Perfect Drug.* I've indicated the answers that applied to Dan's play, followed by my responses to those answers; comments to you, the reader, are indicated in parentheses.

1. *Who and what is the play about?*
(The uncertain future of two brothers.)

2a. *What do the characters want?*
(Again, I always ask the students who have been cast in the play to speak on behalf of their own characters.)
Andrew: "I want to live it up."
Andre: "I want to get my act together."

2b. *Why do you have these needs?*
Andrew: "I want to forget my problems."—Good.
Andre: "I don't want to end up like my dad."—That's a negative want; what's your positive want?
Andre: "I want to live."—Can you be more specific; there is no immediate threat to your life.
Dan: "Andre wants to go to college."—Good! But that's not in the play yet. (Dan makes a note to himself.)

3. *Does this present a conflict?*
Andrew: "I need to be high."
Andre: "I need him to be sober."

4. *How does the conflict get resolved?*
Andrew: "We get high together!"
Andre: "Andrew promises to always be there for me."—So, it's a happy ending? You got what you wanted too, Andre?
Andre: "Not really, I guess. But I seem happy in the end."—Is he happy, Dan?
Dan: "Nah, not really. He's settling for what he can get."—Why does he give up the battle so easily? He even hugs his brother at the end.
Dan: "I don't know. Maybe I should just have Andre leave at the end, run away." (In the moment of *fight-or-flight,* reluctant communicators often opt to bail out on the strong choice that would perpetuate the battle.) —Dan, where would Andre go? If he had options, the stakes in your play wouldn't be very high. Andre needs Andrew to change because he has nowhere else to go. Your current ending is very power-ful because we see Andre get sucked into his brother's lifestyle. You simply have to make him less eager to do so. (As they have been trained to do in acting class, the stu-dents are trying to fill in the character's *backstory*—the motivating factors that are not necessarily discussed in the scene. Although there is no antagonism around the table whatsoever, Dan is quiet. He's heard most of these questions

before and is still ambivalent about revealing the answers. I gently encourage him by focusing only on the holes in his play, and by reminding him that the student actors need his assistance to do their jobs well. I reiterate the Passover Question—number 5 here.)

5. *Why is this conflict erupting today?*

Dan: "Andre is about to graduate from high school and is facing the rest of his life."—Unless he's graduating tomorrow, that's pretty vague. We need a specific triggering event. (Dan is silent, so I suggest that we look for answers in his own text.) We learn that Andre had to carry Andrew home last night—was that the worst he's ever been?

Dan: "He's been bad off, but he never passed out in public before."—Okay, that's great. That would be a strong Trigger for the talk today. Do you all understand the full implications of Andre having to carry his brother? (Three sets of eyes stare blankly.)—Not only isn't Andre getting the parenting he needs, now he has to give it! (They all nod vigorously; they get it.)—And what about you, Andrew, why are you suddenly drinking so much more than usual?

Andrew: "Alcoholism is a progressive disease."—Okay, but that's still not immediate enough. Has a life circumstance changed in a way that is adding stress to your life?

Andre: "Maybe his girlfriend broke up with him."—That would be hard on a guy who's been abandoned so much, but I think this solution needs to come from Dan.

Dan: "He doesn't have a girlfriend. Maybe he got fired, and he hasn't had a job for a long time."—"A long time" isn't immediate enough either. How are they supporting themselves?

Dan: "I don't know. Maybe he just got a new boss who hates him."—Okay, that's a good choice! It doesn't present new logistical problems for the play, and it's credible that a guy who's angry at his dad would have problems with authority figures. (All agree!) —Terrific work everybody. (We all compliment Dan on his play.)

During Table-Work, it is *crucial* that the teacher remain vigilant to ensure that the writer doesn't lose his play in the process of crafting it. I explain to Dan that he is at the point where he has to make a choice about the resolution, including the battle over the cocaine. Andrew can selfishly pursue his own needs by protecting his coke and not his brother. Or he can respond to Andre's cry for help, and try to sober up and become a source of strength and support. When we begin rehearsing the piece, his decision needs to be clear. Dan understands, but he's still resisting. He's afraid of making Andrew seem like a bad guy. I assure him that this will not happen *if he creates* two fully fleshed-out characters.

I then ask the actors if anyone has any last questions for the writer. They raise many of the same issues that I have been raising for months; largely related to the absent character of the dad. Clearly Dan is still trying to tell his story in a way that will allow for an exploration of anger toward an irresponsible parent without completely indicting him. What follows are the questions Dan was asked, and his responses to them:

- Where is the father now?—"I don't know."
- Did he die?—"No."
- Did he abandon them?—"Yes."
- How long ago did he leave?—"A lot of years ago."
- Is he messed up?—"Probably."
- Did Andrew see him get high a lot? Did Andre?—"Yes, they both did."
- Where's the mom?—"The father's drinking caused the marriage, and her, to fall apart." (We all agree that this should be alluded to in the play.)
- Where are the boys living now? (They are unclear here because of the misleading stage direction indicating that the play is set in Andrew's living room.)—"They live together; I only wrote 'Andrew's living room' because Andrew pays the bills." (Dan agrees to clear up the confusion in the next draft.)

This has been a rich exchange of ideas; Dan now clearly has some fixes to make for his next draft. Before he becomes overwhelmed, I invite the other students to take a break then spend a few minutes alone with Dan. I compliment him on his insights, and comment on the apparent commitment of his cast. I then review some other editorial notes with him—those I'd underlined on his last draft. Because this will be an off-book Presentation, he will be asked to give a corrected script to the student actors to begin memorizing next time. I also share some other observations I made while we were reading and discussing the play:

- Did you notice how many times Andre referred to himself as "Andrew"? (Dan nods.) You still need to consider possible name changes.

- Did you notice how awkward Andrew was when he read words like "bro"? And how they both snickered over the bad words? (Dan blushes and nods.) You don't want the Audience to *fall out* of the play; you want them to focus on relationships, not on language.
- Did you take note of any repetitions that could be cut? (He didn't; he was too anxious about everyone liking the play. I point out some of the lines again, and he immediately agrees to edit them; he's starting to feel successful.)

We review all of the other notes on Draft Four, then return to the brother/father confusion. I reiterate that he needs to provide more backstory next time. I again encourage him to commit fully to the choice of having made them two brothers, and not a father and a son. I suggest giving them a more standard age difference, and to let us see how the situation of being abandoned has affected both of them. I assure him that we'll have much more sympathy for Andrew if we see that *he was a victim* of his father's behavior too. Dan says that it's difficult for him to see Andrew that way, but I remind him that a writer must *empathize with all of his characters.* He nods cautiously.

Dan had written something about which he felt impassioned, which he had seized on somewhat unconsciously during a triggered free-write. He is still up against all of the censors that led to his voicelessness in the first place. Although I often have served as an ally in the battle against inner censors, it is not an easy war to wage. Students can remain resistant to change all the way through Table-Work. Some may only be open to making the necessary adjustments after observing a Rehearsal in which student actors' confusion about their characters paralyzes them. Even then, they will probably still defend their previously ambiguous and/or conflicting choices. Sometimes it is not until their second play, often in a subsequent term, that students find the courage to say more. Their courage is usually prompted by witnessing the positive feedback given to those writers whose plays really pay off because the logic of their characters' wants is strongly felt and understood by the Audience.

This was a very successful Table-Work session; Dan's fine-tuning will take one more time. Now that the story questions have been answered, the next session will probably be a one-on-one with me. We will focus on tightening and polishing because there undoubtedly will be both under- and overcorrections. Dan was self-protective but not combative—some new communicators are. Usually, this is because they have felt misunderstood for so long that they can't tolerate being questioned at all, even if it's in the best interest of the play. I usually handle these feedback-phobics by penciling in suggested changes, and then asking them to just listen. If they like the suggestions they can keep them. If not, they can leave the script unchanged, with the understanding that everyone will be confused. Nine times out of ten they agree to make the changes *if* (1) they've been given a choice, and (2) they fully understand the reasons for the changes.

What follows is Dan's final draft; the feedback I gave follows it. I think you will find that while the integrity of his own voice remains in tact, the choices are now far more refined.

Dan's Final Draft, After Table-Work

THE ONLY DRUG

(PUCK and WILL are sitting in the living room. They are getting ready to go out to the neighborhood pub. WILL opens up a bag of coke. PUCK is watching HIM.)

PUCK
I need to talk to you.

WILL
Hang on. I want to fuel up before we
go to the pub.

PUCK
That's what I need to talk to you
about.

WILL
What?

PUCK
You've been hitting it pretty hard
lately. I think you should take it easy.

WILL
Okay "Dad."

PUCK
I'm serious. You need to chill with that
stuff tonight. I don't want to have to
carry you home, like last night.

                    WILL
Worry about your own life, and stop
worrying about mine.

                    PUCK
I'm your brother . . . your life is my life.

                    WILL
That's so adorable.

                    PUCK
I'm being serious.

                    WILL
Don't take me so seriously.

                    PUCK
Stop avoiding the issue.

                    WILL
What issue?

                    PUCK
That I'm younger than you, but I have
to be your parent.

                    WILL
You're a parent to me? Who finished
raising you, and never complained
about it?

                    PUCK
I know . . . and I'm thankful for—

                    WILL
Then stop giving me grief.

                    PUCK
I just don't want you to be like Dad;
turning to some drug when things are
tough.

WILL

That's what you think I do?

PUCK

Yes!

WILL

You don't know what you're talking—

PUCK

(Snaps)

Ever since you got that new boss,
you've been drinking all the time . . .

(HE points to the coke.)

And now you're doing that shit.

WILL

I'm not Dad.

PUCK

I don't want us to be like him.

WILL

It's your choice what to make of
yourself. Don't worry about what other
people's effect on you will be. The
sooner you understand that, the
sooner you'll be at ease.

(WILL snorts another line. PUCK stops HIM.)

PUCK

How can I be at ease? I need you to be
there for me. I need a brother to look
up to.

WILL

I'm not going anywhere. I'm always
here for you; you can look up to me.

                    PUCK
Look at what I'm looking up to . . . a
coke addict and an alcoholic. And I
see myself becoming the same.

                    WILL
Meaning?

                    PUCK
I notice myself drinking a lot for no
reason at all.

                    WILL
And you blame me for that?

                    PUCK
My friends joke around about me
becoming an eighteen-year-old
alcoholic, and it was funny at first. But
it's not a joke anymore, it's weighing
me down. And I don't want to be
weighed down. I want to do stuff with
my life. Time is moving on. I want to
go to college; I don't want to flunk out
of life.

(Silence)

I tried some of your coke last week.

                    WILL
You did what?

                    PUCK
"Coke," "blow," "nose candy"—

                    WILL

(Snaps)

I know what you mean.

                    PUCK
All of the shit I'm talking to you about
now, it just went away. It felt amazing.
I finally felt good about me.

WILL

There isn't anything wrong with you.

PUCK

I'm getting sucked into your lifestyle.

WILL

I never said, "Hey, this stuff is great.
Try it."

PUCK

That's bullshit.

WILL

What?

PUCK

I said that's bullshit! I see you do
things, and then I want to do them
too. You don't have to say anything.

(PUCK picks up the bag of coke.)

This shit is gonna kill us.

WILL

(Tries to get bag of coke)

What the hell do you want from me?

PUCK

I want you to be an older brother who
cares about me.

WILL

I care about you.

PUCK

If you cared about me, you'd stop me.

(PUCK spreads the coke on the table and tries to snort some.)

WILL

Stop it!

(WILL pulls PUCK's head up.)

I said stop it! This stuff is expensive.

PUCK

(PUCK throws the rest of it at WILL. WILL drops to the floor and struggles with the bag, trying to scoop up the remaining coke.)

That shit is all you care about.

WILL

I don't know what to tell you.

PUCK

Tell me that you're going to stop. I haven't had a parent for five years. I need you to really be a father to me now.

WILL

I can't do that.

PUCK

Why?

(Silence)

Why can't you?

WILL

'Cause I'm not your fuckin' father. Your father left you, and your mother gave up on you. And they left me, only an eighteen-year-old kid myself, to raise my little brother. I handled it the best I could.

PUCK

Your best wasn't good enough.

(PUCK rises, starts to leave.)

WILL

You're gonna leave me now too?

(HE grabs HIM.)

Where you gonna go?

(Silence)

We need each other, brother.

(WILL grabs a couple of beers, and holds one out to PUCK.)

Here, have a beer.

(Pause, puts HIS arm around PUCK)
C'mon, we won't go to the pub
tonight.

(HE pushes the beer into PUCK's hand.)

Alcohol . . . it's the number one drug
prevention in the world!

*(WILL smiles at PUCK. PUCK does not smile back. PUCK takes the
beer, hesitates, then drinks it.)*

LIGHTS OUT

Comments on Dan's Polished Play

Dan, I like the title now; it's an ironic comment on the
unhealthy addictions that we can have *to people*. I'm also glad
that you closed the age gap and finally differentiated the
names. However, lest we think that this is a real person who
you might know, I see that you've given Puck a rather fantas-
tical one! You've also answered the Passover Question—last
night was different from all other nights because Puck
became the parent figure. You even gave the brother an
immediate motivation too—the new boss—terrific! Your
responses are all direct now, and you've stayed true to your
original free-write and Treatment: Puck says, "Time is moving
on," and at the end they are "stuck in a moment." The *wants*
are very clear: Will wants his medication; Puck wants a sober
parent. The background information was gracefully included,
and the ending is lovely. We can see that Puck is trapped, as
Will seduces him into getting high. They are both *in-character*
now: the past and present have indeed met. Well done.

Summary

I think it's clear that the tough questions asked during the Table-Work
session brought the *quality of the text up* significantly. That is always
the case, and the subtext will deepen even further during the acting
Rehearsals that follow (see Chapter Five). After much hard work, a
strong play has emerged and so has a strong writer. Both the early

dialogue and story idea had promise; now that promise has been ful-filled. It took a lot of courage on Dan's part, and persistence on mine. Dan resisted most of the re-writes for months, and each re-write revealed another layer and another complication. However, the trust-ing relationship between student and Coach, and the helpful feedback of the group, supported the exploration.

I often develop as much of a relationship with the play as I do with the playwright—I come to know it intimately. All of the answers, and all of the questions, are on those pages. It doesn't have to require exhaustive effort to shape a piece of work, but it certainly requires more than a cursory look. Even if this was the only thing that Dan had written all year, look how much he would have learned about flow, grammar, logic, clarity, persistence, and the fine art of re-writing. I think it would have been well worth any teacher's time.

Dan gained an arsenal of very tangible writing tools. He also learned the most important lesson of all: within him there is a vision that can only be accessed through re-*vision*. Like Grace in the acting class, Dan endured the vulnerability of public sharing in order to experience the triumph of connecting. He watched the arrow find its target—he communicated.

5 Ending on a High Note: Going Public

Over the course of the term that followed Orientation, all of the developing plays were read aloud and discussed in class every week. Students then addressed specific problems in each of their subsequent drafts. Simultaneously, everyone brought at least one Monologue, or a Monologue and a Scene, to fruition. In doing so, students presented them to the group each week, incorporating directorial *adjustments* that deepened the characters and their wants.

As a result of all of this kind of study, students achieve a basic level of craft in re-acting and re-writing, and it is evident in their improved abilities to read, write, speak, and listen. After learning to watch for their problems and improvements, as well as those of the other members of the group, they also achieve an understanding of exactly what those crafts are comprised of. By the end of the course, students become dependent on, vulnerable to, and respectful of one another. They coalesce into a true Company. All of this transformation occurs in the privacy and sanctuary of their classroom.

Now they need to exercise the voices they have found privately, in a public forum. The final Presentation of their original plays offers this opportunity. It is also a celebration, and a reward, for their hard work. Almost every student expresses anxiety about this event, starting at the initial Interview before the term begins, continuing right up until the final Dress Rehearsal. However, if it is handled well, they always wind up elated by the Presentation experience—even hungry for more.

Earning an Audience

I firmly believe that the opportunity to have your work witnessed is a privilege. I emphasize this notion throughout the journey: One must *earn the right* to have an Audience. I think that the professional caliber of the art that this method engenders can be directly attributed to the emphasis placed on the cultivation of real craft, rigorous preparation on everyone's part, and respect for the process, which includes the following:

- Coming to Workshops well prepared for each session.
- Listening attentively while fellow Company members are working.
- Giving helpful and supportive feedback in class.
- Being focused and committed during Presentations.
- Agreeing to answer questions graciously at postperformance Q&A sessions.

When students are Coached to behave professionally during every step of the journey, no great adjustment is needed before going public. They simply have to stay focused on their scene partners and positive wants and then pursue both with energy. It is not easy, however, to *be energetic in the face of terror;* anxiety is very distracting, and very draining. The best *antidote* I know of *is staying connected.* For this reason alone, I have found that it is crucial to move toward going public with group spirit firmly in place, and that the group includes the teacher. It's very easy to allow things such as casting and play selection to become divisive, but I make great efforts to mitigate against this tendency.

The Elements of a Completed Play

Most great writers believe that a play can always be improved on, and for that reason, it is never really finished. In the Find Your Voice™ process, I consider a student piece to have achieved a state of completion when:

- There are two fleshed-out characters with clear wants.
- The wants of the characters are somehow in conflict.
- The conflict gets resolved in some way, not necessarily happily.

- The characters' behavior can be realized on a stage, in realtime.
- The language is clear, and there is flow.
- The Passover Question, why this play had to happen today, is answerable.
- Some relationship to the triggering image is clear.
- Something important to the characters is at stake.

All of these elements are further strengthened during Table-Work, but they should not be conceived from scratch during that limited time. If several of the elements of completion are missing, the play is seen as simply *undercooked*. If only one or two of the key elements are missing, they can be addressed during Table-Work; and, the resulting play may be so much richer that it will seem entirely different.

Being Inclusive

In my early years of teaching this methodology, both at NYU and at the Children's Aid Society, I used to present every piece that was written each time no matter what state it was in by the end of the term. But when all of the plays were presented, and they all had at least two characters in them, it meant that everyone in the Company had the burden of preparing two roles. This was not only far too much pressure for new communicators, but it also made for an interminably long evening for the Audience. For both of these reasons, I abandoned the policy of presenting everything. I also truly feel that the Audience should neither be asked to sit through, nor pay for, work that the presenter knows is not yet ready to be shown.

In recent years, even when a play had power or charm, if it was lacking in more than two of the Elements of Completion just listed, I didn't consider it for public Presentation. This was a tough decision, but ultimately it was far more helpful for the students to see why the plays that *were chosen* worked well. Sometimes the incomplete plays were a result of less effort, and I didn't feel that they should be given an Audience's attention. Sometimes the student worked hard, but wasn't able to get far enough past his or her own resistance to writing more. Interestingly, students who are not presented during their first Trainings almost always go on to write the strongest plays in subsequent attempts, *if the decision not to present* was handled sensitively. This is because their motivation becomes greater, and because they learned so much from watching the more complete plays without the stress of worrying about watching theirs.

In keeping with my desire to give students ownership of the process, if their play isn't chosen, I always outline which elements didn't "gel." The explanation usually comes as no surprise because students come to understand what isn't quite working at any given session. I've learned that most of them have a strong innate sense of quality, and students almost always know it when they encounter a less than complete play. They rarely second-guess the final selections once they're made. My main challenge is to keep the whole Company focused on a strong Presentation, which *requires everyone's efforts.* I also keep reminding them that many of the best writers to come out of Training did not have their first efforts presented publicly. Several of those students later went on to study at some of the country's finest writing programs.

Ultimately, I try to select a Cluster of plays that offers a spectrum of styles, enough casting opportunities for both genders, and some plot variety. In the process, I also try to reward students whose contributions to the Workshop were the greatest. If there are twenty-four students, I select twelve plays. I then cultivate *other forms of inclusion,* if I can. For example, I have occasionally brought in two professional actor friends and asked them to do an in-class reading of the plays that weren't going to be presented to a wider invited Audience. The actors read brilliantly, and the students were thrilled to hear their words come to life in this way. I then had the actors talk about where the student writers might have given them a little more to work with. (If you don't know any professional actors, local theatre companies or colleges are usually happy to oblige.)

Casting

The plays that have been selected for Presentation can now be cast. Casting is a delicate science, and one that must result in the choice of a student who is both physically and temperamentally appropriate for a role. Personally I don't embrace a nontraditional casting approach for *premieres,* even when I direct the work of seasoned professional writers. I think that the first time a piece of work goes public, it should resemble as closely as possible the picture that the writer had in her or his mind's eye. In subsequent Presentations, the director can be more interpretive, after writers have had the opportunity to really see and hear what they originally conceived.

Therefore, I always try to make casting choices that are in keeping with the general descriptions playwrights have provided to me, verbally or in their scripts. Obviously, when working with an *ensemble* of students who are all between the ages of thirteen and twenty-two, some may have to play older or younger than they truly are. But I've found that if they are dressed appropriately, and if they bring total commitment to their work, the Audience believes them to be whatever age they need to be. This is the case on the professional stage as well.

When matching students to the right script, I also seriously take into account the work that I've seen them do in class all term. I ask myself questions such as the following:

- Do they have the necessary sense of humor for this particular portrayal?
- Can they be vulnerable in this way?
- Are they comfortable with the demonstrations of affection or athletic maneuvering called for?
- Are they able to reveal their darker sides as needed?
- Can they handle long speeches, or stage-time alone?

Casting is a whole profession unto itself, so I won't try to pretend this is an easy task. Every student, however, will get to be front-and-center; there are no scenery movers in this process. I do the best I can and then keep in mind that the *Rehearsal process* is a continuation of the learning process. Anything that isn't absolutely natural to the student at the start can be cultivated with TLC.

The First Read-Through

If you have the time to spare, I strongly recommend devoting an hour to having all of the chosen plays read aloud by the students you have cast in them. It's a wonderful way to get the Company excited about the work. It also sets up a vivid demonstration of how far they will come by the time they are presented.

At the first reading of the selected plays, I tell the group about my criteria for the selections I made. I stress the prognosis for future greatness among those writers whose plays were not chosen this time and reiterate the importance of every member's contribution to making the final Presentation a success. Then, I distribute a script to each student; there are no formal auditions and no official *casting notice* is ever posted in advance. I explain that everyone has been *assigned a good role* of similar length, and that everyone will *receive the attention* of the *teacher-as-director* to bring that role to life. There are no winners and no losers. I give students a few minutes to read through their scripts, both to familiarize themselves with the language and to get a sense of the story.

Although they have already heard most of the pieces during the writing Workshops, students may never before have been selected to read a part from the one in which they were cast. For most this will be a *cold reading.* For writers who may have made some major changes during the one-on-one final Polish sessions, it may feel as though the group is hearing something new from them as well. The nervous energy in the room is great; they are all putting themselves out there. For this reason, I have found it to be very effective to point out the group's vulnerability, and that I *am not exempt* from it myself. I want to know that I have pleased students with my casting choices, and to be certain that I have made good play selections. Plays often "sound" very different out loud than they did when read on the page. This is when it helps to remind myself that the plays will *all sound very different*—and much improved—after the Rehearsal period is over.

It is crucial to acknowledge *all the tension* in the room and to pay homage to the fact that it is arising from a *collective desire* to create something of excellence. I urge everyone not to be afraid of anxiety—it can actually be very uniting. I recall one young man, Omar, who was often guarded and disaffected. After his piece was read and the group broke into spontaneous and enthusiastic applause, he dramatically mopped his brow, then smiled and said: "Damn, I was afraid my play would suck and you guys would all hate it!" It wasn't the King's English, but it was an authentic expression of what all of the student writers in the room were feeling. We all laughed until we almost wept, especially because the piece was quite wonderful (see his play, *Girls,* in Chapter Six).

THE COLD READING

Before they begin, I Coach the students on the generally accepted etiquette of cold reading, instructing them to simply read slowly and with intelligence. I then ask the student writers to take notes on any of their own language that doesn't "feel" right to them as they listen; these choices can be addressed further during Table-Work. I also ask them to remain silent and just listen, even if something is misread, though I do jump in if a reader can't pronounce a word. I explain that if readers do misconstrue the writer's intention, it might be a clue that the writing needs clarification. For their part, readers are instructed to simply circle anything they don't understand or don't feel comfortable with; in fact this is their homework for the next session. When the reading is complete, the student actors and writers are applauded by the group and asked to return to their seats.

I have found that some casts read with great connection and passion, and it seems as though they have been rehearsing for weeks. Others will stumble over every other word and never make eye contact. It doesn't matter. Cold reading is a skill that even some professional actors never fully master and some scripts are simply more readily accessible, though not necessarily superior. It all evens out after the Rehearsal period, and I make that fact well known.

After each cast goes up to the front of the circle, in pairs, I announce who the writer is, and then read the title of the play. I also read any salient setting or stage directions such as: "They are in a dark room"; "He picks up the gun, then shoots at his mother"; "It is New Year's Eve"; and so on. This allows the group to make sense of what they are hearing, and to envision what they would see in a full production. What follows is about an hour's worth of reading—twelve plays at approximately one minute per page. By the time all of the plays have been shared, the Company has a sense of the body of work and its collective impact; it is a wonderful lesson in the infinite variety of responses to one given image. Yet, while styles and plotlines vary, almost always inexplicable common elements emerge. One year every piece involved a betrayal of some kind; the Trigger photo had been a broken window! I ask students to listen for the echoes in advance, and they enjoy discovering them. This too helps to mitigate against the inherent tensions of the day.

Establishing Realistic Goals

Depending on the number of sessions your Training encompasses, the plays will ultimately either be read or fully memorized. Rehearsed Readings and fully staged Presentations are very different in scope. However, after many years of presenting both, I have come to hold the opinion that in either case—particularly with new communicators—less is much more. A simple and elegant approach will set off a well-told story just as magnificently as a big-budget production, if the story is in fact well told.

During past years, I have *mounted* many $20,000 Presentations, with teams of designers helping me to create costumes, lighting, sound, and sets. The Presentations often ran for three weeks in fully outfitted professional theatres. More recently, I have opted to mount well-rehearsed Readings with only two chairs and two lights onstage. I can honestly say that while one is unquestionably more visually exciting than the other, the Audience impact of both has been equally profound.

Fuller Presentations require a level of funding that most programs and schools cannot afford and hours of Rehearsals, which most teachers and students in today's test-oriented schools cannot spare. Therefore, in keeping with my emphasis on process rather than product, I have come to feel that a minimal Presentation is a more than adequate way to allow students to go public with pride.

THE BEST OF BOTH

Even if you are working within a very short time frame, you can still incorporate many theatrical elements into Rehearsed Readings. In fact when I train students (or teachers) in a three- or six-week format, we go through all of the same steps as a twenty-four-week after-school program. Five-page plays are developed from a free-write (in response to a photographic Trigger), and they are re-written at least four times. When completed, half are selected and cast from amongst the Company members. They are then given a *one-hour intense* Table-Work/Rehearsal session. During this session, any necessary re-writing—to make cuts, fill in a little backstory, eliminate repetition, *cut-and-splice dialogue,* improve flow, and/or naturalize language—is done on the spot during the first half hour. Toward that end, it is crucial for teachers to go through each script in *advance of the Rehearsal,* recording all questions and suggestions in the margin. This makes the best possible use of the limited time.

By the time the intensive dramaturgical discussion about the script is completed, the student actors will be very aware of the wants and needs of their characters. During the second half hour, using their new Training and your now common language, they can then read the scripts with connection and depth. They can also make additional adjustments as they go, even on the first time through. The second time they read scripts, they can begin to physically act on the characters' behavior. This is where the teacher's homework and preparation is also crucial. I always know which kind of, if any, chairs, benches, or cubes need be onstage; and what behaviors students will need to perform, with a script in hand, in order to fulfill the story. I also determine in advance what, if any, essential stage directions will need to be read aloud. Even during Rehearsal, I read the directions and ask student actors to highlight them in their scripts. If they use a different color than the one they are using to set off their own lines, they will know when to hold for them during the actual Presentation. I try to read as *few* directions aloud as possible because it is difficult for the Audience to hold too many visual instructions in their heads, and hearing directions breaks the flow of the story.

Unlike a *Seated Reading,* in which student actors remain in their chairs reading throughout, a *Staged Reading* implies some movement. If you don't really have the time for any rehearsing, you certainly could opt to have the actors simply remain in their chairs. What is essential is that they read the plays with meaning, authenticity, and connection. This will surely showcase the stories, and some of the Training in acting as well. It may also be the solution that generates the least amount of stress. If there is time, however, I find the Staged Reading to be an ideal way to add a little more dynamic range, while still keeping things relatively simple.

Preparing a Staged Reading

Over the years, I have found it best to focus on several crucial elements during the short Rehearsal that precedes the Staged Reading. Teachers should be sure to do the following:

- Prepare for a quick and intense Polish of the play by studying the script in advance, and then annotating all problem areas and potential solutions.
- Be well prepared to help *explicate the plot* and the characters' wants.
- Listen vigilantly to make sure the student actors are taking the time to really hear and consider what's been said *before they respond.* (Remember, people tend to speak faster when they're reading.)
- Watch vigilantly to make sure that the students are maintaining eye contact, despite the need to periodically consult their scripts. This, more than anything else, will ensure a connected and meaningful performance. I always encourage students to keep a finger near the next line so that they can come away from the page after speaking and then easily return. And if they are listening well, they should begin to know their *cue lines*—the ones the scene partner speaks immediately before their next response.
- Make sure all of this is done with *energy* by reminding students what's at stake for their characters.
- Instruct students to never start speaking until there is light on them, and not to leave the stage until the light has faded—if you are going to be bringing the lights up and down. (This is an elegant way to help focus the Audience and the presenters.)

- Consider the style of clothing students in each play should wear, preferably black and white so as not to pull focus from the stories.
- Know which minimal physical behavior can be included, and note on your script where it should happen.
- Know which props, if any, are essential; have them on hand for the Rehearsal.
- Establish what furniture will be onstage; have a reasonable facsimile on hand for the Rehearsal, and position the pieces as they will be on the stage.

Anything else that you can include will be gravy; the *first six elements* on this list are the meat and potatoes of a successful Reading of any kind. Your greatest emphasis should still be placed on getting students to remain connected and clear on their wants—beginning at Table-Work.

INCORPORATING TABLE-WORK

In both extended and compressed Trainings, the first cold *Read-Through* is followed by the kind of Table-Work session outlined in Chapter Four. At this session, student writers and actors sit at a table with the teacher and scrutinize the play. The intention behind this scrutiny is to make sure that *everyone* involved in bringing this story to life *is telling the same story.* The writer clarifies the story he or she wants to tell so that students can then enact it with assurance and energy.

During Table-Work, the teacher takes great pains to ensure that all of the questions and suggestions are forwarded *in the spirit of helping* the student writer to tell the story in the clearest and most effective manner. The goal is not to critique or re-write the play; the time should be used to fill in any remaining questions about the people, places, or actions represented in the story. The questions should be *challenging;* I have never worked with a student who didn't rise to a Table-Work session that was of very professional caliber. For their part, student actors should focus on fleshing out their characters' backstories, and on clarifying their wants. Student writers should focus on eliminating repetitious language, filling in *plot holes*, replacing language with gestures when possible, and cleaning up *clunky dialogue.* I also make sure that all the information we are given about the characters is appropriate for the story being told. For example, if there is a reference made to a past abortion which has *no* bearing on the reason for the man and woman breaking up, and is never again discussed in the play, we remove it. These random facts are simply "red herrings"; pieces of information that either lead the Audience to the wrong conclusion, or focus them on the story that isn't being told.

THE ACTING REHEARSAL

If Table-Work is productive, you will emerge with a script that has greater flow, more clarity, and *higher stakes.* Student actors will have a feeling of tremendous intimacy with the work by the time the actual *Acting Rehearsal* begins. Although it remains exclusively the student writer's story, everyone in the Rehearsal room should now feel capable of explicating the meanings of the play. Additionally, because cast members have been reading it over and over again to assess the wants and subtexts in every line, they should already be speaking their words with great meaning and connection. In fact, they may have begun to memorize their lines without even trying to.

I usually begin the Acting Rehearsal by asking each of the student actors to once again summarize the story from their characters' point of view, and then to reiterate their wants. This is much like the approach I always used in the weekly re-acting classes that prepared them for this moment. We can then begin the plays' Read-Through with greater energy, which usually will catapult students up out of their chairs. They will begin to *act on* the physical pursuits that they have thus far only identified intellectually. This impulse is good as long as they remain connected to their scene partners, and to their wants. The physicality will actually assist them if they are committing the scripts to memory. If they are just doing a Reading, the Acting Rehearsal can be accomplished within a single hour because only very simple *blocking* will be thrown into the mix. But even that is not so simple because students must remain active and connected with scripts in their hands.

INCORPORATING THE BLOCKING

Once again I will use *The Perfect Drug,* which was analyzed in Chapter Four, as an example. By the time the Table-Work was completed, the confusions that existed in the script had been sufficiently ironed out. The two actors were very clear about:

- Their relationship. [Brothers]
- Their wants. [The younger one wants things to change, he wants a stable home base from which to pursue college. The older one wants things to stay as they are; he wants to escape the responsibilities he'd been handed too early in life.]
- Where they were. [In the living room of the apartment they'd inherited from their absent parents.]
- What was at stake. [Their futures.]
- Why the conflict was erupting that day. [Because the older brother's substance-abuse habit had hit an all-time low the night before.]

When student actors are comfortable with the text, and have had ample opportunity to delve into the behavior of their characters, Rehearsals can focus on the pursuit of their wants. And, because they have already learned how to work well during their re-acting classes, this pursuit should easily translate itself into action. The following are all that the teacher-as-director has to do:

- Consider the staging originally suggested in the script by the student writer.
- Retain the physical impulses the student actors are demonstrating while speaking their lines, if appropriate.
- Respect the parameters of the space and the setting students will eventually be presenting the play in. (In other words, if your stage will be only ten feet wide, students can't rehearse scenes standing twenty feet apart. By the time Rehearsals begin, the teacher should have a good idea about what will be on the stage, and what props students will handle. If there will be no onstage place to sit, students should rehearse standing up, or sitting on the floor.)

Using *The Perfect Drug* as an example again, the addition of physical blocking should serve to further fulfill the play. This can be illustrated in the brothers' fight over the cocaine. Puck is desperate to grab it away from Will, because he views it as a threat to his future. Will is equally determined not to let Puck squander something that he needs right now and that is very expensive. Armed with their full understanding of these wants and needs, the *stakes* should become automatically apparent when the two student actors are handed their prop—a baggie full of confectionary sugar.

At first the new actors had to be pushed into really battling, as opposed to *pretending to battle*. But once committed—the baggie ripped a little and powder went all over the floor—the student playing Will immediately dropped down and began frantically trying to scoop it up. That gesture alone showed Will's desperation more profoundly than any words ever could have, and Dan incorporated the action into his final draft. Similarly, Puck's expression as he watched this desperate act was an equally vivid demonstration of his impending hopelessness. In this manner, the actions were "married" to the words in a most organic way. All the teacher has to do is record it for posterity in the margin of the script. This blocking record ensures that what is discovered during Rehearsal will be memorized and retained. A blocking note might indicate: "Will remains on the floor (after gathering up the coke) for his final confrontation with Puck." This action will enable the Audience to vividly *see how* the younger brother is now going to become caretaker to the older by the very way he looms over him. Each major *action* of the play *should have* a *physical map* of this kind.

Over the years, I have discovered that the toughest page of the script to enact is the first. This is probably because it takes all of us some time to give over to the reality of a play. The antidote to this theatrical *jet lag* is to focus student actors on their behavior rather than on their dialogue. For example, you may recall Dan's addition of the stage direction indicating that the older brother was "fueling up" while the younger brother watched. He gave the first line, "We need to talk," much more depth on paper. This will be true onstage as well; students should be encouraged to take the *time to establish behavior* rather than rush into the speaking of their lines. Watching someone behave is very compelling; students should be assured that it won't be boring. As a rule, at the top of the play I always ask actors to take a moment to *re-act before beginning to speak*.

While proceeding through the script, it is best to continuously follow the guideline that student actors not move unless the action would forward their wants in some way. This was difficult for the student who played Will—he tended to put his nervous energy into wandering. To address this we discussed the fact that drug users are in pain and tend to become completely focused on getting "medications" into their systems. In Will's case the medication was cocaine. He is in his own domain, not under any time pressure to be anywhere. He only wants to focus on getting high so that he can relax. Puck, on the other hand, only finds relief from his tension by interrupting his brother's drug use. This conflict is where both the physical and the emotional tension of the play resides. It comes to life as we see Will focused on his drug, and Puck focused on his brother. The only time that dynamic really shifts is at the very end of the play when Will suddenly realizes he might lose the only family he has left. At that time his focus needs to spread to include his brother in order to get him to stay with him.

This was basically the approach used to block the entire script. We began with the first moment when Puck watches his brother getting high and then screws up the courage to confront him. We ended with the last moment when Will seduces Puck into having a beer with him. Three chairs, which served as the couch in their apartment, were placed in the playing space of the Rehearsal room. I always use the minimum amount of furniture because of the nature of Cluster Presentations. I want the stage to be as uncluttered as possible, and I want the time spent changing over the stage from one play to another to be as easy and brief as possible.

This is true of my use of props as well; they are judiciously chosen to illuminate the actions of the script and to reveal the characters' behavior. In the case of *The Perfect Drug,* all that was needed was the baggie full of powder, a six pack of beer [empty], and a jacket for Puck to grab at the end when he threatens to leave. Three chairs, three props, and some light brought this story very much to life for the Audience. But, to fulfill scripts in this way, students first have to achieve connection, flow, and the courage to battle. Then you as the teacher can prepare to transfer their studio work to the stage; and if you have the time, it may be possible for you to incorporate some higher production values.

Preparing the Presentation

Higher production values can mean simply that students are off-book. Or, there can be some minimal elements of design such as appropriate dress, lights that come up and down, music, and/or furniture. The purpose of these elements is to further ensure that all of the events of the plot can be more fully realized. This does not have to be a costly affair. If the hosting school or after-school organization has access to a space with either *raked seating* for the Audience, or a raised platform for a playing area, everyone involved can either see or be seen. If there is lighting that can be brought up and down to mark the beginning and end of a scene, you can produce a Cluster of short plays with elegance. What is most essential, however, is that the Company be well prepared and well organized. Even if students are going to be sitting in steel chairs on a bare stage and/or under fluorescent lights that never change, they should seem like a "well-oiled machine." And, once they begin to *interact,* they should be completely committed to their scene partners.

Establishing a Running Order for the Cluster

When every play in the entire Cluster has reached the point of readiness, I endeavor to establish the best possible *running order,* which is dictated by many factors:

- Begin and end with the strongest plays so that Audience members feel confident they are in for a good show. They will listen better, and then leave with a strong feeling of closure.
- If any of the students are *double-cast* because someone couldn't see the Training through, don't overtax them; separate those two plays.
- If one of the plays creates a mess on stage—such as the spilled confectionary sugar that served as cocaine in *The*

Perfect Drug—try to end with that one so that it doesn't have to be cleaned up while the Audience sits and waits.

- Alternate lighter and more dramatic pieces, as well as female/female and male/male stories. It is also good to separate any stories whose plotlines are similar, such as brother/brother dialogues or romantic relationship scenes.

As with casting, there are an infinite number of good solutions. After weighing all of the factors I commit to *making* my *choices work.*

The individual plays are rehearsed privately with the rest of the Company using the time to review lines, review blocking, or quietly do homework in another part of the studio. The *Run-Through* is the first time that the entire Company sees all of the fully rehearsed work. It can be as nerve-racking as the first cold Read-Through. The student actors want the writer to be pleased, the writers want the Audience to be pleased, and the teacher-as-director wants everyone to be pleased! This is the time for the teacher to employ a good deal of *fear self-management*, because it is one of the more results-oriented and deadline-bound parts of the process. Fortunately, after practicing fear-management skills throughout the entire Training, teachers have learned to function *despite* all of the anxiety, including their own. And, in so doing, they have modeled what they are most trying to teach.

It takes a lot of trust that the chaos of a first group Run-Through, probably in a new space, will eventually result in order. For this reason, it is often referred to as a *stumble-through.* For Staged Readings, it will be followed immediately by the Presentation. It takes trust, on *everyone's part,* that if the homework has been done well *the rest will fall into place.* Experience is the best teacher of this kind of faith; but even seasoned directors are known to go off the deep end during final Rehearsals. I've found it helpful to lead another discussion about the group's anxiety at this time, assuring everyone that it's normal and that excellent work will result *in spite of it.*

THE FIRST RUN-THROUGH

It is ideal if the Run-Through can take place in the eventual performing space. If it can't the teacher should clear a classroom of chairs; tape off an area on the floor that is the same size as the stage; approximate the placement of the furniture with loose chairs; and have student actors enter, exit, and face the Audience in the same orientation as they will use on the actual stage.

The goal for a first Run-Through is simply to begin thinking of the Cluster as an organic whole and to lay a foundation for *achieving flow.* I usually circulate the running order at the top of the Run-Through, explaining that many factors went into the creation of the order. I urge Company members not to waste time and energy trying to second-guess my choices. Again, the crucial fact is that everyone will be seen and heard in the best possible light. I then seat the Company next to their scene partners in chairs that have been lined up beside the playing area; they are placed in the order of their appearances in the program. Students are then instructed to present their scenes just as they have been doing during Rehearsals, with all of the now established blocking and usage of props.

Before beginning, I give each cast a moment to walk around the playing area. During this time they can get their bearings and adjust to any changes of furniture or spatial arrangements. They may be in a theatre now, as opposed to their classroom, or they may simply be unused to having anyone else but the teacher present to watch them, or both. For most, this will be a disorienting experience. For off-book Presentations, the more confident students may blank out on previously well-memorized lines or movements, and their focus on what they *want* may suddenly disappear. I assure students that it's all normal and temporary, then try to hook them into their scene partners as thoroughly as possible. It is essential to do this on Presentation days as well—they must *only have eyes* for their partners. While performing, their Company, their Audience, and their demons must become secondary. This is for the sake of their nerves, their acting craft, and the stories student actors are there to bring to life.

I also remind them that if they want their invited Audience to sit quietly and respectfully through the Presentation, they will have to begin setting the tone for that today. They are expected to watch each other's work in as nonverbally supportive a manner as possible. I then acknowledge the difficult and good work that's been done up to this point. I also say, "We are now preparing to include the final element that makes a public conversation a conversation: the Audience. Today you are each other's Audience, and the first cast up will have the toughest job of all." This usually provides the most effective antidote to any jealousy that might have been evoked by the running order.

Over the years, I have found that students of all ages are remarkably supportive and proud of one another as they witness a Presentation take shape. They even spontaneously break into applause at the conclusion of each play. While moving from piece to piece, I endeavor to fix any new blocking, *site-line,* or vocal projection problems that emerge in this new and often bigger context. If volume *is* a problem, I encourage the students to pursue their wants with greater energy, rather than simply direct them to speak louder. I also endeavor to get them on and off the stage as quickly and neatly as possible. Toward this end I have students carry on their own hand-held props (for example, the baggie of powder, the six pack of beer, the jacket) and move their own furniture into place. For one play, two cubes pushed together might serve as a couch; for another, they are quickly stacked to serve as a display podium in a gallery. Delegating this responsibility to the student actors not only cuts down onstage traffic, but it also increases their sense of ownership of the Presentation.

Once they have all found their footing, student actors should have gained an understanding of how, when, and where they will enter and exit; what they will be bringing on and off with them; how and where they need to set their stage; and where they appear in the running order. Then, even if they had to call for lines or lost all energy and connection while they worked, the Run-Through will have been a success. I praise students lavishly for their cooperation and courage and reassure them again that any "slippage" is typical and temporary. I close by affirming, "We all have to trust the homework that has pre-pared us for the next moment."

THE DRESS REHEARSAL

Regardless of the simplicity of any lights or sounds that will be used, I always try to determine their placement in advance of the Dress Rehearsal. (In the shorter Trainings, this is held during the second half of the Run-Through, and immediately prior to the Presentation; see the sample schedules in Appendix II). I begin by creating a *Presentation Book* for myself. This is a binder that contains all of the plays, in their proper running order, with tabs that indicate the names of the student writers. I assemble a book for Seated and Staged Readings as well as memorized Presentations, then I decide whether to use any *connective tissue* for the Cluster. I've found that between-the-scenes music really helps to tie the pieces together, heighten the stories, and provide some flow. Although it certainly is not necessary, I particularly like to work with music because the sound of it relaxes both the students and the Audience.

Young people often have music playing in their heads, and it may define a good deal of their life experiences. It is not atypical to have at least one of the student writers ask to use a piece of music prior to, or within, a play. If there is no sound system per se in the Presentation space, I have made this work with as little as a boom-box and a commercial tape or CD. Some of the other songs on a particular tape can even serve as appropriate and ready music for the rest of the Cluster. This can tie a Presentation together beautifully and simply, as well as cover the noise of furniture being shifted onstage. However, having music means someone has to help out during the Presentation, and it takes time to select and label an emotionally appropriate song for each script in advance. Then, at the Rehearsal all the helper has to do is set volume level and determine when to fade the music in and out. Usually this is done once the actors are in place, and the lights are coming up or going down.

Using Your Presentation Book. ■   All of the music "cues" are recorded in my Book, along with the placement of the light cues, prior to beginning. For example, if the room lights are on a dimmer switch, at the top of the Cluster I usually have the Audience sitting in low light and listening to music. We begin when most of the seats in the *house* are filled—always leave some empty seats close to the door for latecomers—and no more than ten minutes past the advertised curtain time, after student actors are in their places. The lights are dimmed, student actors for the first piece come onstage, the music slowly fades out, and the light comes up slowly. The less abruptly these things are done, the more graceful the Presentation will be. My goal is always *seamlessness*—another kind of sustained connection. As with writing and acting, directing requires a mesh of language, actions, images, sounds, and feeling tones that are organically woven together.

This is pretty much the pattern to follow from play to play in a Cluster: lights come down at the end of the scene as the music comes up; student actors exit; next cast enters immediately and gets their furniture into place, and lights come back up while the music fades out. The songs that serve as transitional music may keep changing, and perhaps the look of the furniture as well, but the basic format for the Presentation, as established, stays the same. This kind of consistent pattern not only makes the teacher's job much easier, but it also gives the students the security to focus on their wants without fretting unduly about their itinerary.

All of this should be practiced at the Dress Rehearsal, during which everything must be exactly as it will be when an Audience is present. When all cues have been written into the Presentation Book, and the flow of transitions has been rehearsed, the last elements to be added in are the props—record these too. Once any necessary props have been begged, borrowed, purchased, and collected, they should be laid out on a large table just offstage. Each cast should have a clearly labeled area on the table where things can be assembled. Students are then responsible for retrieving their props before they go onstage, and for returning them to their place on the prop table after they exit. Again, props should be kept to a minimum.

Wrapping Up. ■ For the bow, I usually have all of the students return to the stage in a line rather than bringing them back in discreet casts. This way it doesn't inadvertently become a popularity contest. I also try to have music running "underneath" the bow to heighten the feeling of completion. When the applause is fading, I ask all of the students to be seated onstage to talk with the Audience; all of this should be practiced during the Dress Rehearsal as well. When the entire Cluster has been run-through smoothly with any lights, staging, furniture, props, and/or music, the Dress Rehearsal has been fulfilled. You are ready to Open.

THE BUSINESS OF PRODUCING

Once plays are cast and Table-Work is complete, it is important to focus on two things simultaneously. First is the fulfillment of the Rehearsal process for *each* play, which involves the deepening of acting choices and establishment of blocking, which was previously described. Second is the preparation for the public Presentation of the *entire Cluster* of plays. As all of the rehearsing is going on, the following elements of the business side of any Presentation must be seen to *simultaneously*:

- A Presentation space should be identified and reserved, even if it's the auditorium of your own school.
- A *flyer* should be created to advertise a Presentation to your potential Audience. One idea is to use the photographic Trigger on the sheet(s) you distribute. It can simply be cut, pasted, and copied along with a corresponding title that works for all of the plays. The Cluster that grew out of a photo of a used tea bag was called "Tea Time"; another, which grew out of a photo of a broken umbrella, was called "Rain Dates" (see Sample Flyer in Appendix III too).
- The flyer should be distributed or mailed to the target Audience—families and friends of the students, other teachers and classes in the school, other social service agencies, funders of the program, school or agency officials, and so on—at least two weeks prior to the Presentation.
- If the Presentation is open to the public, reservations should be recorded so that when all of the seats are filled, people can be advised that the performance is sold out.
- A program should be created with the play titles in their proper running order. It should list the cast and their character names, as well as the approximate running time. (On the subject of titles: I've found that students with communication disorders are often reluctant to entitle their works. This is for many of the same reasons that they freeze

up during the Name Game. It requires some sensitive hand holding and encouragement to get certain students to take this final act of responsibility for what they've written. When all else fails, comb the script itself for a short and poignant piece of dialogue that will suffice.)

- Props, if any, have to be collected and safely stored.
- Music and sound effects, if any, have to be acquired or recorded.
- Chairs for the student actors and/or Audience have to be located, collected, and placed.

All of this has to be done on a pre-established schedule so that the preparations for the Presentation will be completed in time for the Opening.

Turning a Presentation into a Dialogue

It takes a lot of courage to write or enact something—to share your interpretations. It also takes a lot of courage to be a good Audience member. In other words, to possibly pay money for something you haven't yet seen, to sit in the dark amongst strangers, to allow others to take centerstage while you sit quietly and anonymously for at least an hour, to honor presenters' victories with applause, and to forgive them their mistakes with patience—all require a spirit of generosity that is rarely exercised anywhere else in life. This is especially true when the material might be challenging, troubling, or uncomfortably familiar.

Because all of this effort is ultimately in the service of finding voices, I invite the Audience to share *their thoughts* during a question-and-answer (Q&A) session following Presentations. For *all levels* of Presentation, this element has long been one of the signatures of the Find Your Voice™ methodology for many reasons, including the following:

- It gives students another opportunity to use their newly strengthened voices in a public dialogue.
- It gives them the ultimate ownership of their accomplishments.
- It keeps the emphasis on process so that the more attention-grabbing "product" doesn't become the end in itself.
- It allows other young people in the Audience to understand that, although the student actors and writers seemed highly accomplished, this kind of achievement is well within their grasp too.

Welcoming the Audience

Earlier in this chapter I touched on the need for fear *self*-management. This is important because, while the move toward public sharing—away from the privacy of the classroom—renders students more vulnerable, it renders teachers more vulnerable as well. Not only will the accomplishments of your students be judged by a wider world, but the world's response also must be carefully managed. For this reason, I always personally welcome the Audience to a final Presentation. I inform members about the nature of the work that they're about to see; for example, original, honest, provocative, sometimes gritty. I also *thank them* for becoming part of the experience.

Preparing the Audience for the Q&A Session

The session following the Presentation requires an even greater level of fear management than welcoming the Audience does. When the lights come up and everyone is ready to step back into their more familiar and often less gracious roles, the teacher must attempt to cull a productive dialogue from an unpredictable and unknown group of people. I often feel like a judge instructing a jury when I tell the Audience that their job is not to provide critiques, which are best left to teachers. Some of what students need to hear from the people who come to a Presentation include the following:

1. Questions about the process: how the plays were written, or how the students prepared for their roles.
2. Questions about, or identifications with, the stories themselves. (I advise the Audience not to ask whether the play is autobiographical; we all write through a personal lens, even if the story is not literally our own.)
3. Comments on aspects of the work that they found particularly insightful or meaningful to them. (However, I ask them not to compare one story to another. This is not a popularity contest—everyone in the Company is a winner.)

Even with stated parameters such as these, Audience members, and sometimes even students, will not always present their better selves. That is why, much like the Workshop environment, it requires so much vigilance to keep a Q&A on track, but *it's worth it.* I usually limit the Q&A session to five minutes, unless the level of dialogue is really rich. The students and the Audience are all fatigued after a Presentation, as am I. However, there is always one particularly loquacious and needy viewer who tries to dominate the conversation. If any one person does go on too long, I politely remind her or him that time is short and that the conversation can be continued privately in the lobby.

As a rule, when Audiences are presented with authentic and well-prepared material, they are quite helpful and appreciative. And, the students, simultaneously high on the victory of having gone public and mellowed by the relief that it's over, are gracious and articulate spokespeople. But it requires stamina and vigilance to manage the *flow between* the two. Often, stamina is not plentiful when you're exhausted from the pressures of last-minute rehearsing, and when you yourself are nervous about the success of the Presentation. While you're not awaiting a *New York Times* review, there's something just as important at stake. You've been assuring your students from day one that they had something to say, and that you could give them the tools to say it well. I have often seen the stress of that responsibility cause some serious backsliding into teaching practices that are less than desirable—both for myself and for others I've trained.

Maintaining Balance

It's all too easy to become punitive with resistant students when the Opening is fast approaching. This may be a time when increased absenteeism, lateness, and unpreparedness can threaten the viability of a positive outcome—for everyone. However, that avoidant behavior is usually due to rising terror. The proper balance of *tough* and *love* needs to be maintained. For example, I try to hang in there as long as possible with a missing student whose courage is flagging, but I might also recruit an understudy from amongst the other Company members. Often this safety net is the very buffer that the reluctant student needs in order to return to full participation.

There are many such buffers that one can apply to lower the growing anxiety level; however, lowering the overall standard of excellence is never one of them. I might simplify the blocking, or eliminate the use of a prop, but I never accept poor focus or a sloppy connection. Again, the most effective method that I have found for dealing with all of the anxiety—students' and my own—is to simply acknowledge that it's there. Like all good Coaches, I give the team a pep talk; when I've named the anxiety for them, it also helps me admit mine to myself. I might say:

> We're all nervous. We've worked hard and we want this to go well. We've also invested in each other, and we don't want to let each other down. The most important thing that

we can all do is to stay focused on the work itself. We'll *all be scared,* in different ways and about different things, but we'll *all survive*—together. We'll probably even enjoy it. And, if the past is any indicator of the future, when we're finished we'll all be proud, and sad that it's over.

FINDING CLOSURE

There are two other traditions that I have consistently upheld for all levels of public Presentation. First, I write an Opening card to each of the students to encourage them as they *battle* their last-minute jitters. In it, I praise them for their accomplishments all term. This is a private communiqué from me to each one and I mean it to be a kind of love letter—not a report card. The purpose, as is the case in professional theatre companies, is to seal the trust between the director and the presenter. It reminds them of how good it can feel to be seen, heard, and known. Students often cry tears of joy as they read these notes.

Second, for the fuller Presentations—if there is the time and budget for it, or if someone knows a photographer who will donate the service—I create a *headshot* of each member. I then hang them on a Company board outside of the Presentation space. This professionalizes the whole affair not only in the minds of the entering Audience, but also in the minds of the new communicators. They are part of a Company; they will be featured in the Presentation; they have learned a craft; they are not voiceless; they are not just a face in the crowd.

EMPIRICAL EVIDENCE OF GROWTH

Gaining the courage to *find your voice,* and the craft to *use your voice* well, are two of the most difficult things I know. Leading others through that process also takes tremendous courage. Your success will not be measured by how well your students perform on a standardized test, but by the level of concentration and commitment in their Presentations on a stage. And, *their* commitment will be mirrored by that of the Audience. This magical dialogue is the live theatre experience, and it is empirical evidence that skills have indeed been acquired. When formerly inarticulate students are clear and connected, you *know they have learned how to speak.* When they listen and *re-act* with intelligence and energy, you *know they have comprehended* what they've read. When their stories are concise and impactful, you *know they have learned how to write.* And, when the acquisition and benefit of these skills is articulated with cogence and respect, you *know they own their newfound craft.* Presentations never happen the same way twice; and with all of the practice and preparation they require, they are always somewhat unpredictable, but they *are always glorious.*

It is almost impossible, especially for those of us who are given to perfectionism, not to worry in advance over every contingency of public sharing. I fret about every dropped line of dialogue, botched piece of blocking, or inaudible punchline. I often feel tempted to apologize to the Audience for everything that *didn't* happen, and then find myself overwhelmed by their amazement about what *did.* Similarly, I am moved by the poignancy of the comments made by even the shyest students during a Q&A. At one recent Presentation, someone asked why all of the plays were so serious. One of the stiffest and most humorless boys in the Company surprised everyone when he answered: "A comic moment is not usually a turning point in someone's life. We only had five pages to establish two people and the conflict they share. In a longer play, there would be room for lighter moments too. Besides, we're teenagers...everything is a crisis!" His graceful and insightful handling of the question allowed everyone in the Audience to laugh, and made all of the feelings that had been stirred up in them easier to bear.

Subsequently, a teacher in the Audience asked a few of the more senior students if the writing gets easier every time. MaryAnn, whose free-write was analyzed in Chapter Two, said: "I've gotten to the point where I know what good writing is; I can even anticipate what the dramaturge is going to say...but it's still not easy. Writing a good play is hard. But I *have learned* to love the challenge."

You may recall my description of MaryAnn as a student who was often paralyzed with self-doubts. She eventually became one of the strongest communicators I've worked with. For me, the "gold" in her statement was the fact that she had *learned* to tolerate the caterpillar phase—the state of becoming; this was because she had experienced being a butterfly—the state of freely being. There are so many butterflies inside of her, and now she knows where and how to find them.

I happened to be sitting in the front row of the Audience during that particular Q&A. It was being led by a former student of mine who is now herself a brilliant Coach (see the profile of Amatullah King in Chapter Six). I'm sure I smiled from ear to ear. Sensing my joy, MaryAnn turned to me and smiled back. We shared a private moment in the most public of arenas. We also shared the pride of her having survived all of the frustrations that almost caused her to give up many times along the way. But like so many others, she had found *her voice.* Now she was going to take it with her to college—and beyond.

6 Profiles of Courage: Teens

I have chosen to introduce this chapter with a profile of an extraordinary young woman who has become pivotal to my ongoing work. Although Amatullah King was one of the shyest students I've ever trained, once she found her voice it was both poetic and powerful. After going on to work at Random House and *Essence* Magazine, Amatullah became my Associate Director, as well as the resident dramaturge for our Trainings. Back in 1993, a member of my Teen Company brought Amatullah to observe a Find Your Voice™ class; the following is what she recalls of that day.

In Her Own Voice

Being a guest, I sat outside the circle of about twenty students from various high schools. I was used to being an outsider, to hiding. I was impossibly shy and awkward, and had trouble looking people in the eye. People had to lean in very close to even hear my voice. As I watched Gail, I was struck by her passion for what she was doing, and her unshakeable confidence in the abilities of the young people who flanked her. She addressed these high school students not merely as teacher-to-pupil, but as artist-to-artist. She challenged the members to "create new visions of themselves," and to develop distinct, eloquent voices through practice and revision. I was fascinated by the acting work, by her painstaking tweaking to craft a motley bunch of memorized words into an organic scene or Monologue. The same intensity could be found in the dramaturgical work, and the revision that went into developing an idea into a complete script.

Watching from the periphery, I had my first internal earthquake. I yearned to be a part of this magic. When the class came to a close, I gathered my courage and walked up to Gail to ask if I could join. She looked into my eyes and said yes. "Yes!" From that moment on, my transformation as a young adult began. I had found a place to test myself, and to emerge from my self-limiting shell of doubt. I learned that I had an ear for language, and a talent for writing. I wrote my first play, and I performed *(gasp)* in front of strangers who, by the end of the Presentation, felt like my oldest and dearest friends.

Since that time, I've wondered what would have happened if Gail had said no. I see the young people out there who don't get that chance—who never hear the affirmation that they are worth the time and effort. I've gone on to other opportunities that my fifteen-year-old self could never have imagined. I attended Cornell University, where I helped to found its first Black Theater Company. And after graduation, I eventually became a journalist at Fairchild Publications, Inc. I also continued my relationship with Gail: as a commissioned playwright for her professional Mainstage, as an assistant Coach with the Find Your Voice™ Program, and as a member of her Alumni Master Class. But most important, I learned to love the cadence of my own voice, and to enjoy the pleasure of making eye contact.

I wish that space allowed for the inclusion of dozens of the plays that have come out of the work using the Find Your Voice™ methodology; the range of styles and stories is immense. But they all have one common thread: In some way, they express the fear of, and the desire for, *connection*. I have selected only two plays, and they reflect very different sensibilities and voices.

I also wish that I could profile all of the hundreds of beautiful young people I've had the privilege of taking this journey with. The striking transformations I've witnessed include these:

■ A student who had been diagnosed as having Attention Deficit Disorder but learned to *really connect* for the first time in his life because of this Training. He was initially so distracted, and distracting, that I contemplated asking him to leave. He ultimately went on to become a professionally produced playwright and has returned several times as a Find Your Voice™ Coach.

- A student who barely said or wrote a word for several terms and then, after writing a breakthrough play (see Figure 6–1), was accepted as an acting major at LaGuardia High School for the Arts.
- A beautiful and gifted young woman, who had great difficulty taking herself seriously, is soon to become an ordained minister.
- An almost inaudible student who was in danger of not graduating from high school, and often did not get out of bed. He now hosts his own Public Access Cable Television show.

They are just a few of the courageous souls who allowed themselves to listen, and to be listened to.

Stacey Robinson's Play

Stacey first took the Find Your Voice™ Training at the age of sixteen. She was already a talented private poet, but was extremely shy and uncomfortable about public sharing. Learning how to write in dialogue form is a great challenge for many poets; they tend to speak primarily in one very personal voice. But Stacey went on to write some truly memorable plays, including the one that follows. In fact, *Being in the Black* was subsequently performed to thunderous applause at an NAACP conference on race relations a few months after we premiered it with the Teen Company.

Although she continued to write during college, Stacey missed having the opportunity to perform as well. So, despite the fact that her comfort on stage was not yet equal to her knowledge of the craft of acting, I suggested that she create a one-woman piece for herself. I knew that she would rise to the challenge. The piece she developed was ultimately produced by the Rites and Reasons Company in Rhode Island. She then had the opportunity to read another of her original pieces on radio station WBAI in New York City. As she was going increasingly public, Stacey continued to work on her skills in my Alumni Master Class during the summers. She was subsequently accepted by Juilliard—for acting! Eventually, she was the first alumnus I commissioned to write for my Professional Mainstage Company. Stacey continues to write and perform nationally.

Figure 6–1. Find Your Voice™ alums Robert Lopez (lyricist/composer of Avenue Q*) and Sarah Paulson (featured in* Down With Love *and* What Women Want*), shown here in the* Ashes, Ashes *Cluster commissioned by Phoenix House in 1992.* ■ *Photograph by Daisy Taylor.*

This play, Stacey's first, was written as part of a Cluster about breakdowns in communication. The unifying Trigger was that of a radio and a set of headphones. (Please note that for the purpose of saving space, stage directions have been run on the same line as the dialogue. For proper play format see Chapter Four.)

BEING IN THE BLACK

by Stacey Robinson

AT RISE: JOHN is sitting on a bench and reading a book. DIANA walks in, looks around, then reluctantly sits down beside HIM, with HER lunch in hand. JOHN is totally engrossed; SHE stares at HIS book, then back at HIM. DIANA removes HER headphones.

DIANA: Hi.

JOHN: (Looks up) Hi. *(Goes back to reading)*

DIANA: (Starts eating lunch) Are you reading *Black Ice* by Lorraine Carey?

JOHN: (Trying not to get engaged) Yes.

DIANA: Is that the book about being a black student at that private boarding school, St. Pauls?

JOHN: Yes.

DIANA: I haven't read it but—

JOHN: You really should pick it up.

DIANA: I should write a book about this place. I'd call it "Being in the Black: The Crisis at the White School." *(Pause)* Have you ever really thought about the name of this school? *(Silence)* The White School of Secondary Education?

JOHN: It was named after the English philosopher, William White. Didn't you know that?

DIANA: Yes, I did. *(Silence)* So, what do you think about the book so far?

JOHN: I just started.

DIANA: No dis intended, but why are *you* reading that book?

JOHN: To gain some insight.

(SHE stares at HIM, waiting. JOHN puts the book down.) I read the articles printed in the school newspaper and to be honest with you, it's very disconcerting that most of the black students here have nothing positive to say about an institution that's so generously providing them with one of the best educations in the country.

DIANA: This institution is generously providing for its black students?

JOHN: Look at the amount of money devoted to scholarships.

DIANA: People of color aren't the only ones on scholarships here. If you're implying that I should be more grateful, and less critical of this institution, just because I'm on a scholarship, you need to think again. *(HE tries to speak but SHE continues.)* Let down your white boy's burden. I'm not some savage subcitizen who's becoming a civilized member of mainstream America simply by the grace of an elite, white school. No pun intended.

JOHN: Don't you think you're being a little melodramatic? *(SHE tries to speak but HE continues.)* Personally I'm grateful to this school for the quality of education it's giving me. In fact, I'm proud of the school, and its basis in the classics.

DIANA: You mean classic Eurocentricism.

JOHN: "Eurocentric" is a buzz-word meaning everything that's wrong with modern education. Our tie with Europe and the whole Western tradition is the reason why ideals like democracy and freedom are held up in America today. *(SHE tries to interrupt.)* Europe was the mother of all of the most important cultural and technological advancements of our time.

DIANA: I'm not trying to deny the merits of the European culture or the American tie with it. Just the perception that no other cultures have made any worthwhile contributions. *(HE tries to interrupt.)* Besides, not all of American history is pleasant. Slavery, for instance, is just as American as apple pie.

JOHN: I knew you were going to bring up slavery.

DIANA: This country was built on the backs of slaves. Why shouldn't I bring them up?

JOHN: I've had this conversation before. I'm tired of being made to feel guilty for a moral crime I didn't commit. My ancestors weren't responsible for the unfortunate treatment—

DIANA: *(SHE interrupts HIM.)* Holocaust! Not unfortunate treatment, a Holocaust.

JOHN: My ancestors were not responsible for the Holocaust of your people. When my grandfather came here, he had nothing. Just the clothes on his back and determination. And he made it. I suggest before you start judging someone else—

DIANA: *(SHE interrupts HIM.)* Wait one second. Was your grandfather white?

JOHN: Yes.

DIANA: And male?

JOHN: Obviously.

DIANA: Then he was halfway there.

JOHN: How dare you disgrace the memory of my grandfather by implying that he didn't have to struggle. I'm Jewish. Black people

aren't the only ones who've had to struggle. You think I can forget my history?

DIANA: I think you can change your name to "Smith."

JOHN: (HE rises.) What gives you the right to be so callous? Am I
supposed to just sit here while you theorize on the evils of all
white people? There have been white people supporting black
people in the idea of equality since the beginning of inequality.
You're not liberated, you're just angry.

DIANA: (SHE rises too.) That's an understatement. Do you know how
many times I've been patted on my head like a dog because someone wanted to feel how different my hair was? Or how many
times I've been told that I'm just here to fill a quota? Do you honestly think that you can ever understand what it's like to be me?

JOHN: Have you ever tried to understand me?

JOHN: *(Simultaneous)*   *DIANA:*
What's the use.   What's the use.

(Both turn to retrieve valuables, and HE starts to exit.)

DIANA: (Sadly) I just want to live.

JOHN: (Turns to face HER, gently) I'm not trying to kill you. *(THEIR
eyes lock.)*

BLACKOUT

Omar Aguilar's Play

Omar took the Training when we were in residence at the high school
he attended. Already in his senior year, I remember wishing I could
have had more time to help him reconnect. He had learned, and very
well, how *not* to communicate. He often didn't show up for class, and
when he did he was rarely prepared. But, once he finally memorized
his Monologue, he really embraced the notion of connecting. Another
somewhat disaffected boy in the class went up as his listener, and
together the two of them found the courage not to laugh at each
other, or at the exercise.

   After Omar got a positive response, and came out from under his
long hair long enough to make eye contact with me, I encouraged
him to bring this same courage to his writing. Up until that point, he
had only managed to write about half a page. Ultimately, and with
much coaxing, he expanded this out to encompass a very complete
interaction. As with his acting, the dialogue was both authentic and
intense. For the first time in his life, Omar began to consider the idea
of becoming an English major. After going on to Hunter College,

Omar returned regularly to our Teen Company Presentations and cheered on those students who were coming along behind him.

GIRLS

by Omar Aguilar

AT RISE: In front of a warehouse in Hell's Kitchen. CHRIS and STEVE are throwing rocks at a factory window offstage.

CHRIS: Yes! You see that? Perfect aim, baby.

STEVE: Yeah! Nice shot. Now watch a pro. *(HE throws. Clank)*

CHRIS: Look at that, you missed. You suck.

STEVE: Whatever, I'm just distracted.

CHRIS: Distracted? *(CHRIS looks around.)* By what?

STEVE: Madeline. I wonder what she's doing right now?

CHRIS: Come on man! This is our time. We're supposed to have fun.

STEVE: Yeah, you're right. Let me try again. *(HE picks up a rock.)*

CHRIS: Good luck, because remember: I'm great and you ain't.

STEVE: *(HE throws. Clank)* Ah, man. I guess I'm off today, so I'll call it a night.

CHRIS: What! Already? *(Looks at HIS watch)* It's only ten thirty. *(Pause)* I know what you're trying to do! You're trying to ditch me, so you can spend time with her.

STEVE: No. Today's just not my day.

CHRIS: Bullshit. I can't believe you're trying to get rid of me by saying your throw is off. You got better aim than me.

STEVE: So what. I wanna spend time with my girl. Is that too much to ask?

CHRIS: Is it too much to ask to hang out with my best friend? I'm always hoping you don't already have plans. And when we do hang out, you seem bored.

STEVE: That's not true. Remember when we chilled that whole week, without once mentioning her name? C'mon, remember? We got twisted.

CHRIS: Wasn't that the week Madeline was being punished?

STEVE: So what man. I'm in love.

CHRIS: How can you be in love at such a young age?

STEVE: I think I'm gonna marry this girl in a couple of years.

CHRIS: Shut up.

STEVE: You've got no idea what it means to be in love. Man, remember when Madeline and I tried to hook you up with her friend? What was wrong with, um, what was her name again? Um, Amy.

CHRIS: Amy? That girl was a ditz. My thirteen-year-old brother was smarter than she was. I mean she was easy, but we had nothing in common. She liked Britney Spears and NSYNC; I like Linkin Park and Slipknot. *(Pause)* And what do you mean I don't know what it means to be in love? Remember when I fell for Michelle? She was perfect.

STEVE: So whatever happened to that?

CHRIS: She was too perfect. We had nothing to talk about because we were too much alike.

STEVE: So what do you want? You want us to hook you up with a girl again? This time we'll make sure that she's your type, but with some differences?

CHRIS: I don't need your help, I can do that on my own. That's not the point. *(Pause)* How long have you known me?

STEVE: Around fifteen years.

CHRIS: How long have you known Madeline?

STEVE: *(Looks at HIS watch)* Three weeks, five days, four hours, and thirty-two minutes.

CHRIS: Loser.

STEVE: What do you want me to do, make a schedule? You're driving me crazy.

CHRIS: You have to start making choices. *(Pulls out a cigarette)*

STEVE: Choices? I already made choices. You're my best friend, and Madeline is my girlfriend. When are you going to make some choices of your own? I been beggin' you to quit smokin'.

CHRIS: Nah, see you caused this. Stressin' me out all the time.

STEVE: Whatever.

CHRIS: And stop trying to change the subject. I wanna know who's it gonna be, me or Madeline?

STEVE: Why can't you be like before? You never had a problem with any of my other girls; you used to understand. What happened?

CHRIS: You weren't as obsessed.

STEVE: Yo man, you have to give me some time to think on this.

CHRIS: You need time to think on this? Come on man, girls come and go, but boys stay together forever.

STEVE: Very heartfelt.

CHRIS: I can't believe you're choosing this trick over me.

STEVE: Watch your mouth. That's my wifey you talking about.

CHRIS: Come on. She's been around, the neighborhood knows about her.

STEVE: Man, you're just sayin' that 'cause you're jealous.

CHRIS: If that's what you wanna believe. *(Silence)* So, choose already! *(Silence)* This isn't a very hard choice.

STEVE: Damn man, it's gotta come down to this?

CHRIS: Yep.

STEVE: All right, fine.

CHRIS: (Pause) So have you come up with your decision? *(Silence. STEVE nods HIS head.)* So spit it.

STEVE: Sorry man. *(Starts to walk away)*

CHRIS: What!! I can't believe you!

STEVE: High school's over. You need to grow up, and get on with your life. *(HE exits.)*

CHRIS: Nah. Fuck you!! *(Throws a rock, hits target)*

BLACKOUT

7 More Profiles of Courage: Teachers

*T*his chapter, containing two teacher plays and two classroom application summaries, is introduced with a profile of an extraordinary educator who has also become pivotal to my ongoing work. Lucy Matos, a Bank Street trained early childhood educator, once thought she could never be a teacher; fortunately, a mentor with the Head Start Program saw her talent. Lucy went on to work alongside education reformer Debbie Meier and to found the much emulated Central Park East Elementary School. She founded the Ella Baker School several years later. Lucy currently serves as a consultant to New Visions for Public Schools for which she is charged with mentoring new principals; she also consults nationally.

Lucy was first introduced to the Guiding Voices™ Training by her District Arts Coordinator when she was trying to galvanize her faculty toward helping students learn in a new way. As is her want, Lucy participated in a Training first before asking it of the rest of her staff. She then participated a second time with her group. I asked Lucy to consider why she—neither a theatre artist nor a theatre teacher—feels that the basic tenets of the Find Your Voice™ methodology are relevant to teachers of any subject; her response follows.

In Her Own Voice

Recently I spent time observing a math class at a small school where I was mentoring the principal. The twenty-five students were seated at clusters of desks. The teacher asked them to take out their homework, and then invited them to go up and write whatever questions they had on the blackboard. No one did, so she asked one of the students to read a problem aloud. She then proceeded to translate what their textbook was challenging them to do. For the next twenty minutes, although the lesson was presented in a clear and sequential manner, only about four students were actively participating. The rest listened passively, at best. And although the teacher demonstrated her knowledge, and was clearly seeking interaction, only one student was regularly asking questions. The principal himself was working on the exercise—and simultaneously *teaching me* how to figure out the problem. We were all involved in the same activity but we were all disconnected—we were a broken circle.

During our follow-up meeting, the principal observed how well prepared the teacher seemed, then shared his concern that the students weren't "getting it." He mentioned that almost one-third of the class was failing, despite efforts to prepare them for the statewide math exam they would take later in the year. The teacher was working hard and, being a math person himself, the principal also had high expectations. The students were coming to class, so what was going wrong? Not one student had accepted the teacher's offer to write on the board. Why not? And, why do students not ask questions when they don't understand? Why does this wall of silence exist between students and teachers, even in a small school? Before my Guiding Voices™ Training, I did not have the specific language to articulate the problem, or the solution.

I return to my observation of the broken circle. In order to make it whole again, we need to manage our students' fears. Math phobias are as abundant in the schools as fears of spoken or written words; and the fear of admitting to "not knowing" crosses all subject areas. *Communication disorders* are a two-way street; they exist between the teacher and the student. We need to reconnect with our students by looking into their eyes, listening to them, and reassuring them. We need to help them take the necessary risks and develop the necessary skills, to take charge of their own learning. This *relationship-based learning approach* helps us become the safe harbors that we want to be. Like doctors, we should have to take an oath: "I promise to take care of the whole child, not just the science, English, or math part." We all want to do well, but we're in too much of a hurry to get there, wherever *there* is. We often leave without the student. There is certainly *urgency*—our dangerously apathetic kids need to be resuscitated. But you can't pump in more air than their lungs can hold. We need to take their pulses, and respond to what *they need*. I have always held these beliefs about good teaching, but before my Training I had never encountered them all in one intense and tangible practice.

What follows are two examples of plays written by public school teachers during their Guiding Voices™ Teacher Trainings. I've included them because I want to highlight the role of the teacher in this experiential learning approach—and how they must *allow themselves to be learners*. The summaries that precede the plays describe the ways in which these two teachers have been applying the methodology in their classrooms. Their approaches are tailored to the time frames and age groups they must accommodate, and provide some alternative perspectives for the college and after-school environments I have documented. Although they teach different subjects, both of the teachers feared public sharing in their own ways. After initial Workshops, they each returned for further Training and were both subsequently invited to teach in my after-school Teen Program.

Again, I wish I could include dozens of examples of the good work that teacher trainees did, and continue to do, including:

■ An automotive mechanic who never planned to be a teacher in the first place. He wound up at a New York City Vocational School and encountered students who "had moved through the system completely detached." His Training not only enabled him to address his own communication issues, but also gave him a tool to motivate and re-engage his students in learning. Most of them didn't have an interest in anything, but he got them writing and listening: "With this methodology I could take kids and gently open them up. They got involved without having to be labeled as shy, or not that smart. After my supervisor observed a few of my sessions, he said that every teacher in the city should have to take this Training—he couldn't believe how much these kids trusted me."

This teacher took the Training twice. His first play was unpresentable—he is now a Coach in our Teen Program. Some other teachers I've worked with are:

- An English teacher who was asked to become her school's theatre specialist, just by dint of her knowledge of Shakespeare. Although she felt completely unprepared for the task, after she took the Training twice she eventually emerged as one of the strongest writers and actors in the group.
- A teacher who prepares students for their GED exams and rediscovered how scary learning something new can be.
- A math teacher who realized that even helping students raise money to start a school store depends on the pursuit of *positive wants*.

These are but a few of the heroes I've had the privilege to learn with, and I am in awe of how wonderfully vulnerable they allowed themselves to be.

Melissa Rocha's Application Summary and Play

Melissa first took one of my Guiding Voices™ Teacher Training Workshops along with four of her fellow teachers from a small New York City middle school that serves bilingual students. Most of the students there come from families that have recently immigrated to the United States, and they tend to lack both craft and confidence in their communication skills. At the recommendation of the school district, the principal hoped to expose a group of her newest teachers to a different approach to improving verbal and written skills. She also hoped to provide them with a common experience, and a common language.

Melissa, who is herself bilingual, was fairly shy and had never studied acting or written a play. She was surprised at how difficult it was to put her work out there. However, by the end of the Workshop, she had gained enough confidence to invite her young students to come and hear the play she wrote, and to see her perform in one during the final Presentation:

> They were so excited and, having done it myself, I became so much more empathetic to *their fears and resistances.* My teaching style has also become more personal; I'm less reluctant to share anecdotes from my own life. I tell my students about how I never raised my hand in class as a kid, and

they're shocked! Now I can even perform my Monologue for them, before I ask them to perform for me.

Melissa returned for a second Training and subsequently taught writing in my after-school program. She then began to lead hundreds of her own students through the methodology; the following paragraphs summarize how she works with students.

I teach Find Your Voice™ to two different groups of students each term during biweekly double-periods. Each group has one session for acting and one session for writing. The first group moves the chairs into a circle, and the second group puts them back. It's a part of their routine and it gives them ownership of the space; routines are very important in middle school. The circle also provides the intimacy of looking at one another, and differentiates this Workshop from their other classes. At first, some of the kids try to hide *behind the circle,* to resist being contained, but I won't give them their time in the spotlight unless they're also willing to join in and listen to the others. Participation in the class isn't voluntary; the school selects homeroom groups of twenty-five that work well together.

During the writing Workshop, a lot of the re-writing is done right there in the classroom, on our computers. I put the students in clusters, mixing the stronger and weaker writers, and they read each other's work aloud. I go from cluster to cluster while the other students in the room practice their Monologues quietly, or write on the computers. If a student is ever really stuck, I work one-on-one. I also collect the drafts and give them additional written feedback because they're young; they aren't always good at recording my verbal comments. (I'm sure I was also much too detailed when I first started out; I didn't yet trust that some things could get fixed later on!)

At first the kids make comments about each other's work like: "That's whack" or "That makes no sense." I tell them that negativity is unacceptable, and then I get them to rephrase comments as questions. By the end of the term, they can really be helpful, rather than just wisecracking. When they do get really into it, they try to emulate the Sample Play in the Find Your Voice™ Manual. They see the class as a special opportunity because I tell them that professionals study the same way.

In the acting class, everyone wants to go up *as the listeners.* And the repeaters from previous terms become the "senior members"— they grow so much. Even the most initially resistant students like it the second time. And the use of Monologues from published plays really raises the bar on their writing. There's so much in those plays to fight for, even though I have to cross out some of the *language.* At first I agonized over choosing the right piece for each student, but then I realized I could always switch if I'd made a wrong choice.

Even though only half of the kids can get up and act each week, it doesn't matter because they love watching each other. Not everyone ultimately memorizes a whole Monologue but they *all establish basic craft,* even if we only focus on the first five lines. They begin to anticipate my comments, and come to understand what *working well* means. Similarly, not all of them write a play with great depth, but they all establish two characters whose conflict gets resolved. I begin the journey with the triggered free-write and Treatment, but I don't do a final Presentation at the end of each trimester. I select the best twelve plays from each term, and [do a Presentation] at the end of the year. I cast them from among *all the actors* I've trained *that year.*

The twenty-four selected actors and I then do some Table-Work and a Rehearsal after school in a Find Your Voice™ club. I try to keep with the protocol, but only about half of the scripts end up typed in proper format. We do have a Dress Rehearsal, wear black-and-white clothes, bring the lights up and down to indicate the beginning and ending of each play, have a flyer with the Trigger image on it, and take a group bow. The entire school comes to the Presentations, and they love it. Even though our big ugly auditorium has terrible acoustics, there isn't a peep in the room.

The kids in the Audience are so passionate about what they see because they are so proud; they all share the same challenges of communicating in a new language. They also relate to the stories; the writing is sincere because the students are all really hungry to express themselves. I remember one boy kept switching his play idea—at first he only wanted to write bloody battles. He ended up returning to his sensitive Treatment about two young basketball players; one of the boys' mother had recently died. Another girl, with a very tough affect, had to be affectionate for her in-class Monologue; she then began to soften offstage as well. They all start to remove their masks.

No matter what subject I teach in the future, I will always use a *Coaching* model. I've learned how to motivate, encourage *practice,* enable discussion, and work through fears. And in my own life, I'm always asking what people really *want* now—I even ask myself!

BREAKING AWAY

by Melissa Rocha

AT RISE: ANA is in HER bedroom in San Juan, nervously packing HER suitcase for New York.

ANA: (Talking to HERSELF while pulling things from underneath bed

and putting them in a suitcase. ROSA enters quietly and watches
with another suitcase.) I haven't seen these shoes in years. *(Look-*
ing around at the pile) I can't take all of these things to New
York.

ROSA: Ana, what are you doing?

ANA: *(Startled that HER MOTHER has come into the room, and nervous*
that SHE may have heard HER) Nothing, I'm just cleaning.

ROSA: You don't need to do that now, we have to leave for the hospital soon. Why don't you help me pack your father's overnight bag.

ANA: Can't you take him by yourself?

ROSA: You're better at talking to the doctors.

ANA: I need to get some things done.

ROSA: You promised you would come. Take out some extra shirts
for you dad.

ANA: *(Going to the closet and pulling out some shirts)* Which one do
you want?

ROSA: Give me both, it doesn't hurt to pack a little extra. *(Silence*
while SHE packs) He's getting sicker, Ana.

ANA: You're just convincing yourself of it by saying that. He'll be
fine.

ROSA: That's not what the doctors said. Anyway I don't have time to
argue, we're running late.

ANA: Ma, I can't stay.

ROSA: You don't have to stay. I just need you to talk to the doctors.
You're the one with the college education. They listen to you.

ANA: I mean I can't stay here.

ROSA: *(Pause)* What?

ANA: I'm getting on a plane to New York tomorrow.

ROSA: When did you decide this?

ANA: At the last minute, because I knew you'd try to convince me
out of it.

ROSA: You can't.

ANA: I've been saving money for a year.

ROSA: You have a responsibility to your family, starting with this
appointment.

ANA: I have to go.

ROSA: Finish packing his bag and I'll meet you outside. I'm not discussing this. *(Heading for the door)*

ANA: *(Grabbing HER)* Listen to me.

ROSA: You don't care if your father gets sicker? You'd leave when he
needs you the most? He's going to the hospital so that they can
clean his kidneys. His diabetes could kill him if he doesn't take
care of himself—

ANA: *(Cutting HER off)* That's just it, if he doesn't take care of himself then there's nothing we can do. If he'd taken care of himself to begin with, he wouldn't be where he is now.

ROSA: If he hadn't worked as hard as he did to make sure you went to college, you wouldn't be where you are either. Have you thought about that?

ANA: About a million times. But how long do I have to keep paying him back?

ROSA: As long as he needs us, and until he's healthy again. *(Turning to leave)* We have to go.

ANA: He should have thought about his health when he was drinking too much.

ROSA: Don't be disrespectful. *(Turning back)* He's your father and my husband. We're all part of the same family. This is where you belong, not in New York.

ANA: I have to live my own life.

ROSA: Now, when I don't have anyone else to help me?

ANA: You have to let go.

ROSA: Your father is going to the hospital overnight.

ANA: They're keeping him overnight just to be safe, not because they think he's gonna die. Don't guilt me into staying.

ROSA: What do you think you're gonna find in New York anyway? Your family's here. New York is someone else's dream, not yours.

ANA: I think I'm the one who should decide my own dreams.

ROSA: Be realistic. Where would you stay?

ANA: Cousin Julia's.

ROSA: Is she paying for your food; getting you a job?

ANA: I'm twenty-five years old.

ROSA: I have enough troubles here, now you want to make me sick worrying about you being in New York?

ANA: New York is a chance to have my own life. *(Pause)* You took a risk when *you* moved away from home.

ROSA: You have a good job here; you don't need to leave like I did.

ANA: I have a good job, but it could be better.

ROSA: Your father won't understand. *(Silence)* You'd be splitting our family apart.

ANA: He already took care of that with his drinking.

ROSA: Don't insult me.

ANA: *(Pause)* I know what I'm doing doesn't make sense to you. And I don't know what I'll find in New York, but I know that if I stay here I'll find nothing.

ROSA: What do you want to find?

ANA: *(Taking HER hands)* The same things you wanted when you left
    your family.
ROSA: My family had no money, I had to find work. You're leaving a
    decent job.
ANA: Didn't you want more?
ROSA: Yes, but you're alone. You're a young woman alone, going to
    New York. I had your father with me.
ANA: I can take care of myself.
ROSA: But I can't take care of your father alone. What am I suppose
    to do without you?
ANA: You'll be fine without me. Dad will be fine too.
ROSA: *(Pause)* When were you going to tell him?
ANA: *(Takes envelope out of HER pocket)* I wrote him a letter.
ROSA: *(Takes it)* He may never forgive you.
ANA: Will you?
ROSA: Why do you have to leave so suddenly?
ANA: Because otherwise you might never let me go. *(Silence)* You
    knew that I would leave one day. I'm not doing it to hurt any-
    one.
ROSA: *(Puts envelope in suitcase)* Get the extra blankets from the top
    shelf in the closet.
ANA: He doesn't need extra blankets, they'll have those in the hospi-
    tal.
ROSA: They say it's cold in New York in the winter. *(After a beat ANA
    hugs HER. THEY embrace for a moment, then ROSA breaks away.)*
    Let's go, we're late. And bring your father's bag. *(Hands HER the
    suitcase and starts to exit)* We'll finish packing when we get
    home. *(ANA stands alone with suitcase.)*

BLACKOUT

Gina DeMetruis' Application Summary and Play

Gina was a highly creative loner, somewhat detached from her colleagues and her work. She first took the Training in a mixed group of
teachers, and subsequently returned to take it again with the rest of
the faculty and the principal of her own school. She is the Drama Specialist at an elementary/middle school that serves at-risk students
citywide, and she harbors dreams of becoming a playwright. She
needed to rediscover her love of writing, as well as her love of teaching. Participation in the Training allowed this dream to flower in Gina,
and consequently in her classroom: "When I first took the Training I

didn't expect much; I thought it was another Board of Education thing. But it reawakened my desire to write, and that hasn't left me since. It's such a straightforward, good approach. It felt a little rigid to me at first, but then I realized that I actually *needed the boundaries*." Following her two Trainings, Gina brought the methodology back to her own sixth, seventh, and eighth graders in the form of a Writing Workshop; here's her summary of how that went.

I essentially took the whole process and tried to duplicate it as part of an enrichment program for students with weak to moderate skills. Each Training was eight weeks long, and I worked with twelve students at a time. For my first Training, I photographed one of the benches in our school playground, and it turned out to be such a good Trigger. I was foolishly worried that there would be no "seeds" for a play—there were!

One boy wrote about a gang having a turf-war over the bench. It was all from his authentic experience—even though he was a quiet and thoughtful guy. At first he just produced a lot of language, with no real idea for any resolution. He had the whole gang onstage, so I asked him to focus on just two guys and why they both wanted that bench. Ultimately he decided that the boys had grown up around there and they both had a sentimental attachment to the bench; their initials were carved on it. In the end, he had the bench accidentally get wrecked during their fight. The play ended with the two boys walking off together. It was very moving.

I made sure that the students stayed with their original ideas, and I used a lot of the Find Your Voice™ terms, such as the Passover Question, wants, and stakes, that are so concrete. After they found their play ideas, we employed the Workshop format, and the students worked on their re-writes by hand at each session. Once the plays were done, I cast and rehearsed them, and had the entire class watch the Rehearsals. We eventually presented all of the plays as a Staged Reading, with just some props. All we had were two chairs onstage, and we brought the lights up and down. The participants' parents, and the other students in the school, all came to see the Presentation. The response was very positive—seeing how their friends had stuck with something and learned to write was so impressive. And, working dramaturgically really taught *me how to listen* with an ear for potential. Each time I teach it I get better. I can honestly say that this is the only Training I've ever [taken and used] that really delivers what it promises.

I initially took Guiding Voices™ for very selfish reasons; I didn't really project an application back to school. But it reminded me that group effort leads to a more personal kind of environment; it reminded me about the importance of *bonding with* my students.

Gina wrote the following play during her second Training, and it was performed to thunderous applause.

CIRCLES

by Gina DeMetruis

AT RISE: ZANE is lying on the couch with crumpled New York Times *spread over HIS face and body. Only HIS feet, protruding at one end, lets us know that a human is present. There is a large bookcase and a door upstage of the couch. ANDREA quietly enters from that door and walks down to the couch. SHE looks at the figure under the papers then sits on ZANE.*

ZANE: Ughh!

ANDREA: I'm sorry. I didn't know there was a life form under all this.

ZANE: Uhhh. *(HE shifts under the paper.)*

ANDREA: You are a life form, aren't you? I wouldn't want to pressure
    you with any high expectations. *(SHE picks up a piece of paper.)*
    This newspaper's from last week. Look, I know "Easy does it" is
    your new motto, but are you supposed to take it so literally? I
    mean, shouldn't you at least change your paper? *(There is no*
    response.) Hey! *(SHE slaps paper.)*

ZANE: I'm trying to sleep.

ANDREA: Well, I admire your tenacity 'cause you've been trying for
    the past forty-eight hours. Not everyone could stick with it like
    that. *(There is no response. SHE gets up.)*

ZANE: Ooof!

ANDREA: Sorry, I don't want to wrinkle my new dress. *(Silence)* I
    went shopping earlier, to celebrate. It's your thirty-first day with-
    out a drink so I bought a new dress. Look. *(SHE does a slow*
    turn, but ZANE remains completely motionless under the paper.)
    The man at the store said it showed off my best assets. I was
    just happy to hear I still have assets. I mean, I'm only thirty-five
    but sometimes I feel a lot older. Now that you're getting sober,
    that'll help. It's gonna rejuvenate both of us. *(SHE pauses and*
    stares at the couch.) Do you think it's too short? The dress?
    (ZANE raises paper slightly and peers out at HER.) Well, it shows
    off my legs. They're still pretty shapely, don't you think?

ZANE: *(HE lets paper drop back on HIS face.)* Do we have aspirin?

ANDREA: You should have seen the guys down the street. I wore the dress home from the store and when I passed those old guys on the corner, the ones who play dominoes, their eyes got so big I thought they'd pop right out of their heads. Their whole board flipped over. *(Pause. SHE deflates.)* Store clerks, old men, and a husband who's buried under last week's newspaper. *(SHE sits down with HER back against the couch.)* Who am I? *(Without looking behind HER, SHE holds out HER hand.)* Could you hold my hand? Honey? Honey! Honey, could you just hold my god damn hand for a minute!

ZANE: I'm trying to sleep.

ANDREA: I'm trying to stay alive! For the past seven years, I've been caught up by this tornado that pulls everything into a frenzy. For seven years I followed your tornado and I've tried to clean up the mess left behind. And now you're getting sober and you come and go from those A.A. meetings like a phantom, then close yourself up in this room. You made me a full partner to your drinking, and now you're getting sober and you shut me out! Where's my payoff? What's in it for me? Say something. Say something! *(There is no response. SHE goes to the door and slams it shut but remains in the room leaning against the wall. ZANE slowly sits up. HE stands and walks a step unsteadily toward the bookcase.)* I'm sorry.

ZANE: *(Shocked)* Shit!

ANDREA: I'm sorry, again. *(ZANE sits back on the couch, visibly shaken.)*

ZANE: Shit. *(ANDREA sits by HIS side.)*

ANDREA: I don't know what got into me. I'm so proud of you. Really, I'm just anxious. *(Pause)* Say something.

ZANE: Nice dress.

ANDREA: *(Playfully through HER tears)* Please hold me. *(THEY embrace on the couch.)*

ZANE: Anything to eat?

ANDREA: Of course. *(SHE doesn't let go of HIM.)*

ZANE: I'm really starving.

ANDREA: *(Letting go)* I'll go fix something. But Zane, come eat in the dining room. Okay? Not in here. Let's eat together.

ZANE: Okay. Call me when it's ready. *(ANDREA gets up with a noticeably lighter physical presence and almost floats past the bookcase toward the door. HE watches HER go, and when SHE suddenly stops, ZANE tenses as HE waits in the silence. ANDREA turns slowly and moves back toward the bookcase. HE looks away.)*

ANDREA: Zane, where were you going?

ZANE: *(Without turning to look at HER)* What?

ANDREA: Where were you going?

ZANE: When?

ANDREA: When you thought I'd left the room.

ZANE: I wasn't going anywhere, I was just standing.

ANDREA: You were heading over here. *(ZANE now turns and looks directly at HER standing in front of the bookcase.)*

ZANE: (Pause) Was I?

ANDREA: You bastard! *(SHE starts throwing books on the floor.)* Where is it? Where is it?

ZANE: (Soothingly) Andrea. Come on, what are you doing?

ANDREA: (Still looking) Where is it? Where is it?

ZANE: (Firmer) Andrea! *(ANDREA turns around holding a bottle of vodka.)*

ANDREA: I knew it! You lying bastard! *(HE tries to pull it from HER hand and a tug-of-war follows.)*

ANDREA: *(Simultaneously)*   *ZANE:*

    You god damn lying bastard!   Give it to me. Let it go!
    (The bottle drops and breaks. THEY both stare at it. Pause)

ANDREA: Well, you could start now, you know.

ZANE: (With humor) It's all right. I've got another one under the couch.

ANDREA: This is not a damn joke. This is our life.

ZANE: Look, I really don't want to have this conversation right now. *(HE walks back to the couch.)* I'll clean this mess up later. You don't have to worry.

ANDREA: I'm not worried about the mess. *(HE lays down and puts a paper over HIS face.)* That's what I do, I clean up the mess.

BLACKOUT

Appendix I

Suggested Monologue and Scene Assignments

MONOLOGUES

Play Title	Playwright	Character/ Gender	Page/ Publisher	Casting Suggestions and Character Wants
A Raisin in the Sun	Loraine Hansberry	Beneatha Female	p. 114 Samuel French	Beneatha's brother has gambled away the money that was going to fund her life-long dream—medical school. She wants her friend Asagai to support her rage. ***Assign*** to a girl with anger who needs a positive want, or someone who has trouble showing anger. ***Want:*** her dream back.
All My Sons	Arthur Miller	Chris Male	pp. 30–31 Dramatists Play Service	Chris has survived the war, but his brother didn't. He now feels too guilty to find pleasure in his fiancée Ann's (his brother's former girlfriend) love. ***Assign*** to a guy who needs to admit needing someone. ***Want:*** to feel worthy of her love.
Amen Corner	James Baldwin	David Male	p. 88 Samuel French	David wants to pursue a career in music, which will entail a life on-the-road, against his mother's wishes. ***Assign*** to a guy who needs to learn both vulnerability and determination. ***Want:*** his mother's permission to leave.
Antigone (Students must work against the stiff language.)	Jean Anouilh	Ismene Female	p. 24 Samuel French	Ismene and her sister, Antigone will both be killed if they defy the king and bury their dead brother. Antigone plans to do it anyway. ***Assign*** to a girl who needs to learn to fight for herself. ***Want:*** to live.
Blood Moon	Nicholas Kazan	Manya Female	p. 45 Samuel French	Manya was date-raped and decided to avenge the rapist by feeding him the dead embryo in his dinner. When she reveals this, she needs to know she's not considered crazy. ***Assign*** to a girl who needs to connect to others. ***Want:*** affirmation.

PLAY TITLE	PLAYWRIGHT	CHARACTER/ GENDER	PAGE/ PUBLISHER	CASTING SUGGESTIONS AND CHARACTER WANTS
Children of a Lesser God	Mark Medoff	James Male	p. 67 Dramatists Play Service	James is married to a deaf woman who refuses to learn to speak. He won't agree to "make a baby" unless she makes more of an effort to be independent. (Remember that the "listener" can't hear the speaker unless she can *see* his lips.) **Assign** to a guy who has trouble connecting (very physical piece). **Want:** his wife to communicate with him more.
The Colored Museum	George Wolfe	Normal Female	p. 47 Broadway Plays	Normal is emotionally abused by her mother. After a miscarriage she fantasizes about being the first girl to ever lay an egg, and tries to get the audience to see it. **Assign** to an outgoing girl who needs to admit her vulnerability. **Want:** to be seen as special.
Crimes of the Heart	Beth Henley	Babe Female	p. 31 Dramatists Play Service	Babe was married off at a young age to a much older bully of a man. Because she had seen her mother battered into suicide, she takes a more aggressive stance. **Assign** to a girl who needs to take more responsibility. **Want:** to stay out of jail.
The Dark at the Top of the Stairs	William Inge	Sammy Male	p. 40 Dramatists Play Service	Sammy was sent to grow up in a military academy and, therefore, never felt wanted. He is meeting his best friend's sister. **Assign** to a shy guy who needs to connect. **Want:** for his blind date to like him.
The Days and Nights of Beebee Fenstermaker	William Snyder	Beebee Female	p. 34 Dramatists Play Service	Beebee has been frantically searching for herself, and hasn't yet admitted that she needs other people. Her best friend is about to move away, so she is demanding that God help her learn to find "connection." **Assign** to a girl who needs to admit anger. **Want:** help to find love.
Death of a Salesman	Arthur Miller	Biff Male	p. 15 Dramatists Play Service	Biff needs his family's approval, but doesn't want to be like them. **Assign** to a guy who needs to connect. **Want:** his brother's permission to leave.
The Diary of Anne Frank	Dramatized by Goodrich and Hackett	Anne Female	p. 97 Dramatists Play Service	Anne's family is in hiding from the Nazis. There is only one person her age there, and he is depressed. She needs to fend off her own feelings of hopelessness. **Assign** to a girl who needs to connect. **Want:** Peter's companionship.

Play Title	Playwright	Character/ Gender	Page/ Publisher	Casting Suggestions and Character Wants
Does a Tiger Wear a Necktie?	Don Peterson	Linda Female	p. 39 Dramatists Play Service	Linda is tired of being pigeon-holed as a loser . . . a "drug addict." She wants to be seen as someone who has been in pain and managed to survive. *Assign* to a girl who needs to raise her self-esteem. *Want:* respect.
The Dreamer Examines His Pillow	John Patrick Shanley	Donna Female	p. 13 Dramatists Play Service	Donna's boyfriend has been cheating on her and is starting to fall apart: She wants him to stop treating her the way her father treated her mother. Her tough language is the way she really talks. *Assign* to a girl who needs to loosen up and fight for herself. *Want:* her boyfriend's love.
The Dreamer Examines His Pillow	John Patrick Shanley	Tommy Male	pp. 15–16 Dramatists Play Service	Tommy has cheated on his girlfriend and now doesn't want to lose her, but he's having a breakdown and can't explain his behavior. *Assign* to a guy who needs to learn to fight for himself, or one who needs to admit vulnerability. *Want:* his girlfriend.
The Effect of Gamma Rays on Man-in-the-Moon Marigolds	Paul Zindel	Janice Female	p. 39 Dramatists Play Service	Janice wants to compete with her brainy sister by winning the science competition. She inadvertently horrifies the audience with the grizzly details of her experiment. *Assign* to a girl who needs to take herself more seriously . . . must be done "dead pan." *Want:* to get attention for winning.
Extremities	William Mastrosimone	Marjorie Female	p. 33 Samuel French	Marjorie managed to stop her attempted rapist and now wants to kill him. To do so she must prevent her roommate from calling the police. *Assign* to a girl who has trouble expressing anger, or a girl who doesn't watch for a response well. *Want:* help to avenge her rapist.
Glass Menagerie	Tennessee Williams	Tom Male	pp. 25–26 Dramatists Play Service	Tom feels trapped at home with his widowed mother, and his sister is handicapped and fragile. *Assign* to a restless spirit who needs to connect. *Want:* his sister's approval for leaving home.
Glass Menagerie	Tennessee Williams	Jim Male	p. 59 Dramatists Play Service	Jim has been unwittingly brought home to a dinner with his friend's unmarried sister. He wants to build up her self-esteem before he confesses that he's already engaged. *Assign* to a confident guy who doesn't listen well. *Want:* to let her down easy.

Play Title	Playwright	Character/ Gender	Page/ Publisher	Casting Suggestions and Character Wants
Glass Menagerie	Tennessee Williams	Tom Male	p. 24 Dramatists Play Service	Tom has always felt trapped by his widowed mother, and tries to get her to see how controlling she's been by exaggerating. **Assign** to a guy who has trouble expressing anger. **Want:** his freedom.
Inherit the Wind	Jerome and Lawrence Robert Lee	Rachel Female	p. 111 Bantam	Rachel's father has been prosecuting Burt for teaching his beliefs about evolution. She loves Burt and wants to help, and she also wants to find her own freedom from her father's oppression. **Assign** to a girl who needs to take a stand. **Want:** her independence.
Ivanov (Students must work against the stiff language.)	Anton Chekhov	Sasha Female	p. 81 Signet	Ivanov is depressed about the recent death of his wife and feels unlovable. Sasha must convince him that he is all the more attractive to her because he needs her. **Assign** to a girl who needs to connect, or to a girl who needs to admit vulnerability. **Want:** to have her love accepted and returned.
Manchild in the Promised Land	Claude Brown	Claude Male	pp. 122–123 of novel Simon and Schuster	This is the story of Claude's struggle to survive the streets of Harlem. **Assign** to a guy who has the capacity to rise above the streets. **Want:** a chance to make it.
Night Mother	Marsha Norman	Jessie Female	p. 50 Dramatists Play Service	Jessie has never felt like she had the right to her own life; she plans to commit suicide to make her mother pay for her being oppressed. **Assign** to a girl who has trouble expressing anger. **Want:** to end her pain and hurt her mother.
Nuts	Tom Topor	Claudia Female	p. 82 Samuel French	Claudia was raped by one of her "Johns," who she then murdered. She is on trial and wants to plead self-defense. Her mother wants her to plead "insanity"—she doesn't want the world to know that Claudia became a hooker. **Assign** to a girl who needs to fight for herself, or to a girl who needs to focus her anger. **Want:** to prove her sanity and go free.
Of Mice and Men	John Steinbeck	Curley's Wife Female	pp. 61–62 Dramatists Play Service	Curley's wife is secretly asking Lenny—a retarded but strong farmhand—for protection. **Assign** to a girl who needs to connect. **Want:** help to escape from her abusive husband.

Play Title	Playwright	Character/ Gender	Page/ Publisher	Casting Suggestions and Character Wants
Of the Fields Lately	David French	Ben Male	pp. 1–3 Samuel French	Ben, who never appreciated his father when he was alive, now pines for the relationship they never had. **Assign** to a guy who needs connection, or to a guy who needs to admit vulnerability. **Want:** forgiveness.
Saint Joan	George Bernard Shaw	Joan Female	pp. 137–138 Penguin	Joan is to be given life imprisonment for "witchcraft" because she has heard God's voice. Her former followers have not fought for her to be set free. She has been betrayed and wants them to fear the choice they've made. **Assign** to a girl who needs to learn to fight for herself. **Want:** her freedom.
The Shadow Box	Michael Cristofer	Agnes Female	pp. 59–60 Samuel French	Agnes needs a social worker at the hospice to understand why she has been lying to her dying mother about her sister's death. **Assign** to a girl who needs to feel accepted. **Want:** to keep her mother alive.
The Shadow Box	Michael Cristofer	Mark Male	pp. 70–71 Samuel French	Mark's lover, Brian, is dying of cancer and he needs Brian's ex-wife to stop pretending he's going to recover. **Assign** to a guy who needs to learn to fight for himself. **Want:** help coping with his impending loss.
Slow Dance on the Killing Ground	William Henley	Rosie Female	p. 41 Dramatists Play Service	Rosie recently had sex for the first time with a boy she didn't know well, and ended up pregnant. She shares this with a waiter at a coffee shop on the way to have an abortion. **Assign** to a girl who needs to feel accepted. **Want:** support for her decision.
The Star Spangled Girl	Neil Simon	Sophie Female	p. 20 Dramatists Play Service	Sophie demands that the superintendent of her building stop stalking her. **Assign** to a girl who doesn't take herself seriously, or to one who has difficulty showing anger. **Want:** to be left alone.
Wonderful Tower of Humbert Lavoignet	Lynne Alvarez	Mike Male	pp. 8–9 Broadway Plays Publication	Mike's father is in a catatonic state, but Mike believes that if he keeps trying he can reach him. **Assign** to a guy who needs connection. **Want:** a response.

SCENES

Note: The two characters' wants are always in conflict.

Play Title	Playwright	Character/ Gender	Page/ Publisher	Casting Suggestions and Character Wants
All My Sons	Arthur Miller	Sue (S)/F Ann (A)/F	pp. 36–39 Dramatists Play Service	Ann's fiancé, Chris, lives next door to Sue and her husband. Chris has come back shell-shocked from the war, but Ann needs to believe he's a good man. *Assign* to girls who need to fight *for* things. *Want:* (S) to control their husbands; (A) to believe her husband doesn't need to be controlled.
Antigone (This is a modern adaptation on an ancient play; language can seem stiff . . . work against it.)	Jean Anouilh	Ismene (I)/F Antigone (A)/F	pp. 22–26 Samuel French	King Creon has made an example of Ismene and Antigone's brother by killing and refusing to bury him. Antigone plans to save his soul; Ismene is too scared. *Assign* to girls who need to learn to fight. *Want:* (I) to obey king and live; (A) to defy king and risk death.
Between Daylight and Boonville	Matt Williams	Marlene (M)/F Carla (C)/F	pp. 71–76 Samuel French	Marlene doesn't acknowledge her husband's affair; Carla urges her to change her life. *Assign* to girls who need to express anger. *Want:* (M) her family and small-town life; (C) to break out.
The Children's Hour	Lillian Hellman	Karen (K)/F Martha (M)/F	pp. 64–67 Dramatists Play Service	After being accused of being gay, Martha admits that she is. Karen does not share her feelings. *Assign* to students who need focus and work on intimacy. *Want:* (K) to run from the truth; (M) to face it.
Crimes of the Heart	Beth Henley	Babe (B)/F Lenny (L)/F	pp. 63–68 Penguin	These two sisters receive a visit from a third sister, Meg, whom they haven't seen in a long time. Right now, Babe needs Meg's help. *Assign* to one introvert and one extrovert who need to connect. *Want:* (B) (extrovert) to defend her sister Meg; (L) to condemn Meg.
The Crucible (This is an "imitation" period play . . . language can be stiff . . . work against it.)	Arthur Miller	Proctor (P)/M Abigail (A)/F	pp. 141–145 Bantam	Proctor and Abigail have had an affair. She wants to continue, he does not. Although he still desires her, she has threatened his wife's life. *Assign* to students who need help physicalizing. *Want:* (P) to save his wife; (A) to betray his wife.

Play Title	Playwright	Character/ Gender	Page/ Publisher	Casting Suggestions and Character Wants
The Crucible	Arthur Miller	Proctor (P)/M Elizabeth (E)/F	pp. 47–53 Bantam	Proctor has cheated on Elizabeth, and she doesn't believe that the affair is over. She still needs him to prove himself; he needs to be trusted again. **Assign** to students who need to work on subtext. **Want:** (P) to be forgiven; (E) to expose his guilt.
The Days and Nights of Beebee Fenstermaker	William Snyder	Beebee (B)/F Nettie Jo (N)/F	pp. 28–34 Dramatists Play Service	Nettie has come to tell Beebee that she's leaving; Beebee doesn't admit that she needs her to stay. **Assign** to girls who need physical work. **Want:** (B) to hold on to her friend; (N) to get married and move away.
Death of a Salesman	Arthur Miller	Hap (H)/M Bif (B)/M	pp. 12–18 Dramatists Play Service	These two grown brothers have come together to discuss their ailing father. Hap would like them to become a tight family again, but Bif can't forgive his father. **Assign** to guys who need to connect. **Want:** (H) to stay together; (B) to leave their father.
Effect of Gamma Rays on Man-in-the-Moon Marigolds	Paul Zindel	Ruth (R)/F Tillie (T)/F	pp. 31–34 Dramatists Play Service	The girls are preparing for a science contest that Tillie usually wins... Ruth tries to undermine her. **Assign** to girls who need to learn to fight. **Want:** (R) to win contest; (T) to win contest.
The Glass Menagerie	Tennessee Williams	Laura (L)/F Jim (J)/M	pp. 54–61 Dramatists Play Service	Jim has been brought home to meet his friend's sister, Laura (they don't know that he's already engaged); she is extremely fragile. **Assign** to a girl who needs to be drawn out, and to a guy who needs focus. **Want:** (L) to feel desirable; (J) to let her down easy.
Golden Boy	Clifford Odets	Joe (J)/M Lorna (L)/F	pp. 27–31 Dramatists Play Service	Joe is a prizefighter who dreams of being a musician; Lorna is his manager's girlfriend who's been sent to get him to keep fighting. **Assign** to a guy with pent-up anger and to a girl with hidden vulnerability. **Want:** (J) to quit fighting; (L) him to fight.
Hatful of Rain	Michael Gazzo	Celia (C)/F Johnny (J)/M	pp. 57–61 Samuel French	Johnny has returned from Vietnam with a secret drug addiction; his wife Celia is pregnant and fears that he's cheating on her. **Assign** to a girl and guy who need practice connecting. **Want:** (C) the truth; (J) to hide the truth.

Play Title	Playwright	Character/ Gender	Page/ Publisher	Casting Suggestions and Character Wants
Hatful of Rain	Michael Gazzo	Polo (P)/M Johnny (J)/M	pp. 41–44 Samuel French	Johnny has become a heroine addict in the war and keeps borrowing money from his brother until "he can quit." He now owes money to the local dealers. *Assign* to boys who need to sustain focus and positive wants. *Want:* (P) to stop enabling brother; (J) money for drugs.
Hooters	Ted Tally	Cheryl (C)/F Rhonda (R)/F	pp. 31–35 Dramatists Play Service	These friends have taken a vacation alone together before Cheryl gets married. Cheryl would like a last fling, but Rhonda is not comfortable with guys. *Assign* to girls who need to battle (physical scene). *Want:* (C) to party; (R) time alone.
In the Boom Boom Room	David Rabe	Chrissy (C)/F Susan (S)/F	pp. 74–81 Grove Press	Chrissy was sexually abused as a child and needs advice on how to deal with men; Susan is gay and attracted to Chrissy. *Assign* to girls who need to connect. *Want:* (C) a female friend; (S) a female lover.
Laundry & Bourbon	James McLure	Hattie (H)/F Elizabeth (E)/F	pp. 12–18 Dramatists Play Service	Elizabeth's husband has run off and doesn't know she's pregnant. Hattie wants her to tell him so he'll stay put, but Elizabeth doesn't want to trap him. *Assign* to girls who need to work on connection. *Want:* (H) her friend to have the same life she does—kids and an unexciting marriage; (E) romantic love.
Loose Ends	Michael Weller	Susan (Su)/F Selina (Se)/F	pp. 61–64 Samuel French	Susan is pregnant and needs Selina's support for having an abortion. Selina longs for a family and doesn't understand her friend. *Assign* to girls who have trouble expressing anger. *Want:* (Su) advice on her marriage; (Se) out of her friend's affairs.
Loose Ends	Michael Weller	Susan (S)/F Paul (P)/M	pp. 74–82 Samuel French	Paul confronts his wife about an abortion she never discussed with him. She thinks he only sees a "baby machine"; he thinks she doesn't love him enough to have kids. *Assign* to a boy and girl who need to work on intimacy. *Want:* (S) to know she's enough without a baby; (P) a baby to demonstrate their love.

Play Title	Playwright	Character/ Gender	Page/ Publisher	Casting Suggestions and Character Wants
Savage in Limbo	John Patrick Shanley	Linda (L)/F Savage (S)/F	pp. 9–16 Dramatists Play Service	Linda just got dumped by her boyfriend; Savage has never had one. Savage needs to lose her virginity; Linda needs to reclaim her innocence. **Assign** to girls who need to work on listening skills. **Want:** (L) to learn to live without a man; (S) a social life.
Summer and Smoke	Tennessee Williams	Alma (A)/F Nellie (N)/F	pp. 66–69 Dramatists Play Service	Nellie tries to gain the admiration of her former teacher by telling her she's engaged; Alma has to cover the fact that Nellie's fiancé is the man she's always loved. **Assign** to girls who need work on subtext. **Want:** (A) to run away from her sorrow; (N) to share her joy.
Top Girls	Caryl Churchill	Joyce (J)/F Marlene (M)/F	pp. 88–93 Samuel French	Many years ago Joyce agreed to raise her sister Marlene's illegitimate child; now she fears that Marlene will take her back. **Assign** to girls who need to express anger. **Want:** (J) her family as it is; (M) a new role in Joyce's family.
View From the Bridge	Arthur Miller	Catherine (C)/F Rodolfo (R)/M	pp. 45–48 Dramatists Play Service	Catherine's uncle has convinced her that Rudolfo only wants to marry her to gain citizenship. **Assign** to a boy and a girl who need the discipline of connecting and practice with intimacy. **Want:** (C) him to prove his sincerity; (R) her to just trust him.
The Wager	Mark Medoff	Honor (H)/F Leeds (L)/M	pp. 53–59 Dramatists Play Service	Honor has a need to seduce men; Leeds doesn't want to succumb, but he's lonely and attracted to her. **Assign** to a boy and girl who fear intimacy. **Want:** (L) to protect himself from being hurt; (H) to conquer.
When You Comin' Back Red Ryder?	Mark Medoff	Angel (A)/F Stephen (S)/M	pp. 7–11 Dramatists Play Service	Two long-time friends work in a restaurant together; he pretends he doesn't need her, she wants him to admit that he does. **Assign** to students who need to coordinate physical action with dialogue. **Want:** (A) to cement their friendship; (S) to deny their friendship.

Appendix II

Two Sample Schedule Options

OPTION 1

Find Your Voice™ Teen Training Program
Six-Week Intensive, With Rehearsed Reading (20–25 Students)

SESSIONS	ACTING	WRITING
1	Read 1st Monologue (*Orientation)	Free-Writes
2	1st Monologue off-book	Treatments
3	1st Monologue deepens	1st Drafts
4	1st Monologue deepens	2nd Drafts
5	Final Presentation of Monologue	3rd Drafts

Play Selection and Casting

6	Rehearsal/Table-Work of plays	Polish Plays
7	Dress Rehearsal/Presentation of Rehearsed Reading and Q&A	

OPTION 2

Find Your Voice™ Teen Training Program
Twenty-four Weeks, With Off-Book Presentations (20–25 Students)

SESSIONS	ACTING	WRITING
1	*Orientation	Free-Writes
2	Read 1st Monologue	Treatments
3	1st Monologue off-book	Revise Treatments
4	1st Monologue deepens	1st Drafts
5	1st Monologue deepens	2nd Drafts
6	Read 2nd Monologue or Scene	3rd Drafts
7	2nd Scene or Monologue off-book	4th Drafts
8	2nd Scene or Monologue	5th Drafts
9	2nd Scene or Monologue	6th Drafts
10	2nd Scene or Monologue	7th Drafts
11	Rehearsal of best Monologue	Polish Drafts
12	Dress Rehearsal/scene night	Final Play Due

Selection and Casting of Plays

	ACTIVITIES
13	Read-Through of Plays
14	Table-Work
15	Table-Work
16	Table-Work
17	Acting Rehearsals
18	Acting (off-book)
19	Acting (off-book)
20	Blocking Rehearsals
21	Blocking
22	Group Run-through
23	Run-through
24	Dress Rehearsal and Evening Presentation

*All sessions are three hours long

Appendix III

STARFISH THEATREWORKS, INC.

FIND YOUR VOICE
Teen Training Program
presents

AN EMPTY CHAIR
AN EVENING OF ONE-ACT PLAYS
(inspired by the photo below)

Andrea Sperling

ten plays written and performed by:

Khiratullah Abdul-Haqq
Alex Abell
Paloma Allen-Davis
Morgan Benson
Alana Christian
Rosa Collazo
Kefáh Crowley-Abdelhay
Dahvid Doré
Christina Freeman
Sarah Goldstein

Rachel James
Erin Ortiz
Joseph Pisani

Tiffany Taylor

Suann Thompson
Jasmin Torres
Josephine Vella
André Zucker

ASSISTANT TEACHERS	DIRECTOR	DRAMATURGS
Sharifa Hayle*	Gail Noppe-Brandon	Laura Castro
Abdul Rasheed*		Jeanette Horn

*Graduates of the *Find Your Voice* Teen Training Program*

Wednesday, June 3rd, 1998 at 1 PM & 7 PM
Clark Studio Theatre
The Samuel B. & David Rose Building, 7th Floor
70 Lincoln Center Plaza (corner of 65th St. & Broadway)
Admission: $5 / $1 Students
Please Call 212.741.9868 for reservations

STARFISH
theatreworks
one vision • many voices

TWENTIETH
500
VOICES
FOUND
ANNIVERSARY

www.starfishtheatreworks.com

149

Glossary

Achieving flow—Process by which lines and Scenes transition seamlessly from one to the other.

Acting—Doing or behaving as another; a physical choice.

Acting for your own enjoyment—Playing emotions with no regard to the desired outcome, or to the response of the listener.

Acting Rehearsal—Time used to focus on behavior rather than text.

Adjustment—A direction that, when applied, will alter or strengthen physical behavior, wants, or subtext.

Advisory—Unstructured time period during the school day.

Aligned—A state in which the body is evenly held and presented.

Ally—A teacher who advocates for the students and helps to fight their communication demons.

Authenticity—A quality of writing and acting that is truthful.

Backstory—Background information or motivating factors that are not disclosed within a Scene or Play.

Battling—The act of fighting for what you want, and the basis of all good drama.

Blanking out—Forgetting a line in the script.

Blocking—Physical movements.

Calling for a line—When a student blanks out and requests a prompt from whoever is holding the script.

Casting notice—A public list of roles and the students who have been selected to fill them; not used in this methodology.

Cause-and-effect relationship—(1) The logic of a response; (2) the relationship between assertions and behavior.

Character differentiation—Making sure that everyone in a Play is a fully fleshed-out and unique individual.

Checking out—When a student actor is disengaged; simply waiting for their own next turn to speak.

Choices—What we write as writers; and how we, as actors, interpret a character's behavior.

Cinematic pans—A camera technique that allows the viewer to see a vast location.

Close-reading—Analyzing a Play.

Close-up—A cinematic technique for viewing one particular character or object as if very near to you.

Clunky dialogue—Language that is awkward for the actors to speak.

Cluster—A group of thematically linked Plays.

Cluster approach—The presentation of several short thematically linked Plays which offer substantive roles for all participants.

Coach—A teacher who uses motivation and fear management to form relationships with learners.

Coaching—Inculcating skills while providing moral support.

Cold reading—Reading text aloud that you've never seen before.

Collective unconscious—Symbols and responses that all peoples share.

Commenting—Inappropriately using your face to telegraph the meaning behind your words.

Communication demons—The particular internal blocks that keep someone from learning and communicating; can result in poor eye contact, lack of focus, fear of touch, and so on.

Communication disorders—Blocks that prevent people from truly connecting with others.

Communicatively disabled—Anyone possessing an inability to connect fully with others. This disability can demonstrate itself in things such as extreme shyness, functional illiteracy, academic failure, depression, social alienation, hyperactivity, or Attention Deficit Disorder.

Company—A group of people who share a common purpose.

Conflict—What results when the wants of two characters are in opposition.

Connecting—Truly seeing and hearing another person; admitting the desire for a response from someone.

Connective tissue—(1) Lines in a Play that respond to or elaborate on previous ideas; (2) design elements that provide flow and continuity to a Cluster of Plays.

Conservatory-style—Professional level.

Contact Sheet—A list of the participants in a Company, and a way to contact them.

Containment—The effort to safeguard student privacy and concentration by maintaining a listening environment.

Context—Whom a character is talking to, what the character wants, and why she or he wants it.

Craft—Highly refined skill.

Creative play—The process of revising written pieces through imaginative problem solving.

Cross Cultural Clustering—Bringing together diverse participants to create collections of works reflecting a range of human stories.

Crossing a bridge—When an actor takes the time needed to process new information and then makes a decision.

Cue lines—The dialogue your Scene partner speaks immediately before your next response.

Cutting-and-splicing dialogue—Interspersing two long, consecutive speeches into single lines of responsive dialogue.

Dark sides—Our less than admirable feelings and traits.

Dead fish-eye syndrome—The appearance of making eye contact; looking without really seeing.

Dialogue—Two characters speaking and responding.

Doing nothing—Pursuing wants through listening and connecting, without over-acting.

Double-cast—When one student is in two different Plays within a Cluster.

Drama queen—One who over-acts.

Dramatic tension—This results when conflicting wants are pursued.

Dramaturge—A playwriting Coach; a specialist in the art of dramatic writing and re-writing.

Dramaturgical Inter-Play—When the dramaturg taps into the writer's imagination to find an idea for a Play.

Dress Rehearsal—Time used to practice for the final Presentation with costumes, props, lights and sounds, just as they will be when the Audience is present.

Echoes—Overlapping ideas in student free-writes that are written in response to the same Trigger; reflective of a collective unconscious.

Empathy—An understanding of, and patience with, other people's fears.

Energy—The fuel necessary for acting—doing.

Engaged—Being fully connected to another; committed to a pursuit. It is the antidote to anxiety and alienation.

Experiential learning—Attaining skill by doing.

Explicate the plot—Describe the basic story.

Exposition—Background information about characters, or story, which is simply told to us.

Extended battle—The dialogue in a Play that furthers the character's ability to fight for what they want.

Falling out—A situation in which the Audience is no longer actively engaged in the Play's story.

False voice—A tone that is imitative or melodramatic rather than authentic.

Fear management—Providing encouragement and a safe environment to students in order to Coach them past their fear of public sharing; having them connect to another person and then embracing their efforts.

Feedback phobic—People with such a fear of negative judgment that they can't tolerate questions or comments.

Fight-or-flight—The moment in a Play when the writer can choose to consummate the battle between the characters, or resort to having one of the characters run away.

Fighting for—When an actor pursues a positive want, on behalf of themselves or another.

Find Your Voice™ methodology—A process that teaches someone to communicate through trust and the attainment of craft.

Flow—(1) Sustained pursuit of a want; (2) a quality of seamlessness.

Flow of logic—The purpose behind the character's words in a Scene or Monologue, an understanding of which enables the memorization process.

Fourth wall—A theatrical term that refers to the open space between the stage and the Audience; in a classroom, it is the space between the two students who are working and the rest of the class.

Free association—Connection between two things that are linked in the writer's mind.

Free-write—The process of writing whatever comes to one's mind, without editing or self-censoring, in response to a prompt or Trigger of some sort; most often a photo is used for this methodology.

Getting stuck—Forgetting lines.

God is in the details—A reminder to use specificity to enrich story.

Golden Rule—No one may laugh at anyone's attempt to communicate—ever.

Guiding Voice™—A Coach who leads others to develop their voices.

Hamburger helper—Extra dialogue added to a Play simply to make it longer without actually forwarding the wants of the characters or developing the plot.

Hammering—Overemphasizing words rather than trusting the Audience to understand the material.

Headphone-itis—A symptom of the need to block out others and remain disengaged.

Headshots—Photos of students' faces, which can be posted outside of the Presentation space.

Healing relationship—One that's based on trust and nurturing.

High stakes—The urgency with which a conflict must get resolved.

Hit-and-run syndrome—When a student briefly makes eye contact while speaking a line and then immediately looks away, thereby missing the response.

House—(1) The space in which the final Presentation takes place; (2) the Audience, as opposed to the stage.

Illiteracy—The inability to communicate effectively, or to effectively receive the communication of others due to a communication disorder.

In-character—When a student actor's behavior is in keeping with the wants of the Play.

In the flow—The student who knows what his or her character wants and actively pursues it from their Scene partner—total engagement.

Inkblot—The suggestive quality of a visual Trigger that often elicits an unconscious response.

Instrument—The student's body, emotions, senses, and thoughts.

Integrated approach—Studying re-writing and re-acting simultaneously.

Intellectual improvising—Spontaneously responding to a dramaturg's questions during Inter-Play.

Inter-acting—Allowing the listener time to answer, even if he or she has no lines.

Inter-Play—See Dramaturgical Inter-Play.

Interview etiquette—A gentle way of introducing potential participants to the methodology.

Issues—The things students shy away from.

Jargon-addiction—A symptom of the need to disguise one's authentic voice—and therefore not be judged—via overuse of slang.

Jet lag—The time it takes to give over to the reality of a Play.

Jump-cuts—The cinematic technique of moving from one location to another instantly.

Key line—A phrase in a free-write that suggests a potential plot, a character, or a conflict.

Learning circle—A placement of chairs in which all participants are both teachers and learners of each other, and in which all can make eye contact.

Letting go of the words—When a student's lines are so well internalized that her or his full focus is on their character's actions.

Level playing field—A class where everyone addresses their own limitations.

Lines—Words that a student's character speaks.

Listener—The person who is being spoken to during a Monologue, and from whom the speaker is seeking a reaction.

Listening—The act of extreme connection; it requires all five senses.

Listening environment—A space in which one can concentrate and remain focused.

Losing your Play—Making changes that are not in keeping with the original idea for the Play.

Manageable solution—Feedback that is clear and focused enough for a new writer to implement.

Manual—A written introduction to the Find Your Voice™ methodology.

Monologues—A series of lines that are uninterrupted by another character's verbal responses.

Name Game—When each of the group members assigns themselves descriptive names; a way to begin being seen and heard.

Naming—When the teacher articulates and understands anticipated negative reactions.

Negative want—A character's desire to not accomplish, or not attain. Shuts down action.

Nonlearners—Students who are no longer open to the communication of teachers; that is, refuse to participate.

Obstacle—An impediment that keeps a character from achieving his or her want.

Off-book—When a student actor has completely memorized his or her script.

On-book—(1) When someone is holding and following along on a script to aid another student if she or he blanks out and calls for a line; (2) when a student reads from a script.

On their feet—When students physicalize their Scenes.

Open—When the student's eyes, chest, and body are ready to give and receive information.

Orientation—A time for students to get used to a new environment and/or a new set of ideas.

Other-conscious—When the focus is taken off of the self so that a response can be sought. It enables connection and counteracts stage fright.

Over-actors—Students who are working too hard at showing what they feel rather than pursuing what their characters want.

Overcorrecting—When a student changes too much in response to an adjustment that has been suggested.

Ownership—What is acquired when the teacher's adjustments are fully understood by the student.

Pacing—The rhythm of a Play, which is dictated by the student's heartbeat or adrenaline in response to the intensity of the situation and the urgency of the character's needs.

Partnering—Using another student as a listener during the performance of a Monologue.

Passover Question—Why the Play had to happen today.

Personal habits—Student behavior that impedes the realization of the character's wants—for example, mumbling, avoiding eye contact, racing, and so on.

Physical map—A record of how the actors' movements explicate their wants.

Physicalize—To demonstrate a want through behavior.

Planted—When a student's full weight is evenly distributed on two feet—that is, they are ready to act.

Plot holes—Information that is missing from the Play.

Polish—A final draft, with correct grammar and format.

Polluting—Giving feedback that tells the student writer how to solve the problem.

Positive want—A character's desire to accomplish or to attain rather than to not accomplish or not attain; emphasized in this methodology.

Premiere—The first time a Play is presented.

Presentation—An opportunity to go public.

Presentation Book—A director/teacher's record of all the Plays in a Cluster, in their running order and with all cues indicated in their proper places.

Prior circumstance—The moment before the Play or Scene begins; it provokes the first line.

Private expression—Writing that isn't shared.

Production values—Elements that dress the Presentation, i.e., lighting, costuming, sets, music.

Profanity—Gratuitous language that disrupts the flow of the story and causes the Audience to fall out.

Prop table—The offstage prep site for all handheld items that will be used by the students during a Play.

Public sharing—Speaking, or having your words spoken, to others.

Pulling—The art of acting to try to get a response.

Pulling focus—A negative behavior that draws attention away from the student who is speaking.

Racer—Someone who speaks the lines of his or her character too quickly to be absorbed by the listener.

Raked seating—When the Audience is on an incline so that they can see the stage.

Re-acting—The art of responding to the person you're listening or speaking to.

Read-Through—An unrehearsed reading of a Scene, Monologue, or Play.

Realtime—When the theatre Audience sees everything as it happens.

Red herrings—Misleading plot clues.

Rehearsed Reading—A rehearsed but not memorized Presentation of a Play.

Relationship-based learning approach—Embracing students by guiding and Coaching them through a personalized experience.

Resolution—How the conflict between characters is settled; not always happily!

Revision—The art of honing your original idea to make it stronger—raising the stakes, strengthening continuity, eliminating repetition and exposition, simplifying language.

Re-writing—Solving the problems that arose in a previous draft by adding or changing text.

Rule of three—A technique to help student writers sustain conflict by never letting a character get what he or she wants until it's been asked for at least three times.

Running lines—When students speak their lines to each other to assist in memorization of a Scene.

Running order—The order in which the Plays will be seen at the final Presentation.

Run-Through—A Rehearsal that takes place without stopping.

Ruptures in connection—When the listener disengages, forcing the speaker to pursue the connection with renewed vigor.

Scene—A self-contained portion of a full Play.

Scoring—Rehearsing lines with a particular manner of delivery in mind rather than allowing the spontaneity of the listener's response to dictate the tone.

Seamlessness—A quality of flow in acting, writing, and directing.

Seated Reading—Student actors remain in chairs while reading their scripts.

Settings—The locations of the action in a Play.

Show—don't tell—A plea to demonstrate a character's state of mind through some form of behavior, rather than expositional text.

Showing—An off-book performance of a Scene or Monologue, after which the students receive a teacher's feedback.

Site-line—An Audience member's view of the stage.

Social distance—The comfortable amount of space needed between two students to achieve intimacy and connection, without either encroaching.

Stage directions—A writer's instructions about the characters' physical behavior.

Staged Reading—A rehearsed and physicalized presentation of a Play that is not memorized.

Stage-time—The duration of the student's part in a Play.

Stakes—The urgency with which something is needed or desired.

Stretching—Working on material that allows a student actor to explore traits he or she is not yet comfortable with.

Stumble-through—The first time a cast rehearses all of the Plays in their running order, often in a new space.

Subtext—The underlying motivation for the words spoken in a Play.

Table-Work—The time prior to Rehearsal, in which the students and teacher sit at a table and clarify character motivation, backstory, and plot; usually this results in further re-writing.

Throwing away lines—Speaking the dialogue of a Play in a manner that renders it devoid of meaning.

Time frame—The period during which the action of the Play takes place.

Treatment—The summary of a Play that includes who the characters are, what they want, how those wants are in conflict, and how the conflict gets resolved; it serves as a contract for new writers to fulfill.

Trigger—Pictorial image or theme that can speak to anyone; used as a point of departure to generate writing.

Triggering event—The reason for conflict in a Play.

Trusting relationship—What is established when a Coach successfully manages students' fears.

Turnkey teaching—Enabling others to teach the methodology independently.

Under-actors—Students who can't sustain connection, and who lack sufficient energy to pursue wants.

Undercooked—A Play that does not demonstrate all the elements of completeness.

Understudy—A student who learns another student's part in case she or he needs to cover—perform the part—because of the other's inability to be onstage for a Presentation.

Unintended self-disclosure—When a student writer becomes too autobiographical.

Unison—Lines or music that is performed simultaneously by more than one person.

Universality—When a story captures a widely felt human truth.

Unjustified—Actions or results that don't seem to grow organically out of the plot.

Unmotivated movement—Physical actions that do not forward a character's want.

Upstage—The part of the stage that is the farthest from the Audience, which a student actor tries not to face.

Urgency—The immediacy with which a want or need must be met.

Voicelessness—The state in which a person has lost the ability to communicate effectively; usually for fear of negative judgment.

Wants—The desires that motivate a character's actions.

Warm-ups—Exercises that ready the body and/or voice for communicating.

Wings—The offstage areas where students, props, and costumes wait unseen.

Working—When students are performing Scenes or Monologues.

Working too hard—(1) When a student tries to illustrate words by pointing; (2) telegraphing attitudes with facial expressions.

Working well—When a student is completely focused on the other person and what he or she wants from that character, and thus is able to override self-consciousness.

Workshop approach—When students witness and participate positively in each other's learning process.